Lecture Notes in Energy

Volume 82

Lecture Notes in Energy (LNE) is a series that reports on new developments in the study of energy: from science and engineering to the analysis of energy policy. The series' scope includes but is not limited to, renewable and green energy, nuclear, fossil fuels and carbon capture, energy systems, energy storage and harvesting, batteries and fuel cells, power systems, energy efficiency, energy in buildings, energy policy, as well as energy-related topics in economics, management and transportation. Books published in LNE are original and timely and bridge between advanced textbooks and the forefront of research. Readers of LNE include postgraduate students and non-specialist researchers wishing to gain an accessible introduction to a field of research as well as professionals and researchers with a need for an up-to-date reference book on a well-defined topic. The series publishes single- and multi-authored volumes as well as advanced textbooks.

Indexed in Scopus and EI Compendex The Springer Energy board welcomes your book proposal. Please get in touch with the series via Anthony Doyle, Executive Editor, Springer (anthony.doyle@springer.com)

More information about this series at http://www.springer.com/series/8874

Stéphane Goutte · Khaled Guesmi ·
Raphaël Homayoun Boroumand · Thomas Porcher
Editors

Advances in Managing Energy and Climate Risks

Financial, Climate and Environmental Sustainable Strategies

Springer

Editors
Stéphane Goutte
CEMOTEV, UVSQ
Paris-Saclay
Guyancourt, France

Khaled Guesmi
CRECC
Paris School of Business
Paris, France

Raphaël Homayoun Boroumand
CRECC
Paris School of Business
Paris, France

Thomas Porcher
CRECC
Paris School of Business
Paris, France

ISSN 2195-1284 ISSN 2195-1292 (electronic)
Lecture Notes in Energy
ISBN 978-3-030-71402-4 ISBN 978-3-030-71403-1 (eBook)
https://doi.org/10.1007/978-3-030-71403-1

This Springer imprint is published by the registered company Springer Nature Switzerland AG
The registered company address is: Gewerbestrasse 11, 6330 Cham, Switzerland

Preface

The energy sector is complex and characterized by a radical uncertainty. It combines geopolitical, economic, environmental, technological and social dimensions. The overlapping of decisions at the international, national and local levels contributes to the complexity of energy systems. Under these conditions, implementing an ideal policy combining security of energy supply, industrial competitiveness, and the fight against global warming while preserving the purchasing power of consumers is a real puzzle. In addition, there are endogenous (economic and financial crises) or exogenous (health crisis such as the COVID-19) shocks to the economy which can postpone detrimentally the implementation of sustainable energy policies.

The role of economic researchers is to provide sound policy recommendations through economic analyses, case studies and applied modelling to guide public and private decision makers for relevant and sustainable energy and climate policies.

This is the purpose of this book which brings together a dozen of researchers who work on topics notably related to climate change resilience.

Several aspects of energy and climate risk management are analyzed, notably the exogenous crisis of COVID-19. What are the determinants of an effective green energy development strategy? What are the impacts of COVID-19 on renewable energy projects? What are the effects of oil price volatility and COVID-19 on power companies? How the volatility of oil and gas prices affects CO_2 emissions? What is the impact of energy price regulation on energy consumption and efficiency? Do smart grids have a sufficient impact to contain CO_2 emissions?

To answer these questions, the authors carried out case studies in several countries (USA, India, and MENA countries) and made international comparisons (USA, Japan, China). This book contributes to characterize several major energy risks, particularly in periods of crisis. This risk characterization is a prerequisite before implementing sustainable energy and climate policies.

Guyancourt, France — Stéphane Goutte
Paris, France — Khaled Guesmi
Paris, France — Raphaël Homayoun Boroumand
Paris, France — Thomas Porcher

Contents

Contributors

Narjess Aloui University of Tunis Carthage-Carthage Business School, GEMAS Lab, FSEG, Tunis, Tunisia

Amine Ben Amar International University of Rabat, RBS College of Management, Rabat, Morocco

Razan Amine Johns Hopkins University, SAIS, Washington, DC, USA

Sonia Arsi University of Carthage-Carthage Business School, Tunis, Tunisia

Ahmed Ayadi Center of Research for Energy and Climate Change (CRECC)-Paris School of Business, IHEC Carthage, University Paris 8, Tunis, Tunisia

Fateh Belaid Faculty of Management, Economics & Sciences, Lille Catholic University, UMR 9221-LEM-Lille Économie Management, Lille, France

Sihem Ben Saad Carthage Business School, University of Tunis Carthage, Tunisia, Tunisia

Khouloud Senda Bennani UTC, Carthage, Tunisia

Elias Boukrami Faculty of Business and Management, Regents University London, London, UK

Sahbi Farhani Assistant Professor, Department of Economics and Quantitative Methods, Higher Institute of Finance and Taxation of Sousse, University of Sousse, Sousse, Tunisia;
QUARG UR17ES26, ESCT, Campus University of Manouba, Manouba, Tunisia

Yosra Ghabri University of Tunis Carthage-Carthage Business School, Tunis, Tunisia

Rafla Hchaichi University of Tunis Carthage-Carthage Business School, ESCTRA Lab IHEC, Carthage, Tunisia

Soumaya Ben Khelifa University of Carthage-Carthage Business School, Tunis, Tunisia

Hela Mzoughi University of Tunis Carthage-Carthage Business School, ESMA-Higher School of Statistics and Information Analysis, Tunis, Tunisia

Imen Sdiri Carthage University, ISG Bizerte, URCC Lab, FSEG, Tunis, Tunisia

Renewable Energy in the MENA Region: Key Challenges and Lessons Learned

Fateh Belaid, Elias Boukrami, and Razan Amine

Abstract Many pieces of evidence showing that investments in energy transition can boost GDP and create jobs. Further, national and regional energy transitions can help build resilient economies and societies. Therefore, linking short-term actions to medium- and long-term strategies is vital to achieving the Paris agreement on climate change the Sustainable Development Goals (SDGs). In this context, this analysis aims to explore the key challenges and lessons learned regarding the development of renewable energy. The setting of the current study is the MENA countries, as examples of growing economies, most of them experiencing extensive economic and energy reforms. First, we briefly review the demand for renewable energy and the resources available, before examining some of the challenges that need to be addressed to meet deployment targets. Second, we present some case studies to show what is at stake in some countries, the challenges, and the lessons learned. Aggressive RE policies seem to be vital to achieving key energy-policy goals, and the so-called "multiple benefits" of RE in the MENA region, such as addressing climate change and air pollution, improving energy security, and increasing energy access. Policies should be more ambitious to address national challenges and targets and strengthen climate commitments. However, securing strategic financing, investing in transition-related infrastructure, diverting investment from fossil fuels, and making bailouts conditional on climate action should be a cornerstone of national strategies.

Keywords Renewable energy · Economic development · Economic growth · Sustainability · MENA

F. Belaid (✉)
Faculty of Management, Economics & Sciences, Lille Catholic University, UMR 9221-LEM-Lille Économie Management, F-59000 Lille, France
e-mail: fateh.belaid@univ-catholille.fr

E. Boukrami
Faculty of Business and Management, Regents University London, Inner Circle, Regent's Park, London NW1 4NS, UK
e-mail: elias.boukrami@regents.ac.uk

R. Amine
Johns Hopkins University, SAIS, Washington, DC, USA

S. Goutte et al. (eds.), *Advances in Managing Energy and Climate Risks*,
Lecture Notes in Energy 82, https://doi.org/10.1007/978-3-030-71403-1_1

1 Introduction

Energy is an indispensable catalyst for economic activity and a source of comfort and well-being for every individual in the World. In recent years energy demand experiencing a steady increase, well below the usual traditional increase that the world economy has witnessed the last five decades. As a result, reducing energy consumption has been placed on the political agenda of most countries around the world. Demand almost doubled over the period 1990 to 2014 (BP 2017). This demand is driven mainly by economic growth, with an average growth of 2.5%, and significant population growth, which rose from 5.3 billion in 1990 to 7.3 billion in 2014 (BP 2017).

The current trajectory of global economic development is not without consequence on our planet and this is alarming. According to a recent report,[1] anthropogenic emissions of greenhouse gas as a result of human activities are responsible for almost 95% of global warming. In the absence of a reinforcement of the international action in favor of the climate, the rise of the average global temperature could reach 2 °C resulting in even more natural disasters (floods, droughts, degradation of the agricultural yields, accelerated melting mountain glaciers, and polar ice caps, rising sea levels, etc.) and irreversible effects on ecosystems.

To address the underlying problems, the global energy sector is experiencing profound and rapidly accelerating change. Accordingly, investment patterns are changing as a result of a multitude of factors, including changing consumer preferences, technological change, and policy measures. Policies affecting change in this sector are driven by a series of objectives. Besides the high consideration given to climate change, energy policy-makers over the World focus on other priorities, including (i) enhancing energy security; (ii) warranting affordable energy supply; and (iii) ensuring universal access to energy and enhance environmental quality.

The traditional fossil energy system is in deep crisis. Centuries of dependency on fossil fuels have led to severe environmental damage and centralized generation, distribution, and power structures from which only a few countries that benefit. Energy transformation should be part of a fundamental paradigm shift towards a sustainable development model. Socially acceptable and ecologically sustainable solutions have to be sought to improve the energy supply, the overall industrial production, the transport, and the heating sector.

Various ways have been identified to reach a low carbon development path (see Fig. 1), including (i) changing individuals practices and behaviors; (ii) improving energy efficiency; (iii) improving carbon sinks by reducing deforestation and increasing the use of bioenergy with carbon capture and storage; and (iv) enhancing the use of low carbon and non-carbon energy.

The latest instrument, renewable energies, can offer a sustainable, development-promoting, and cost-effective alternative to the current fossil energy system (Tiba and Belaid 2020, 2021; Mongo et al. 2021). In addition, the possibility of creating wealth

[1]IPCC. (2018). Global warming of 1.5 Degrees. Retrieved from https://report.ipcc.ch/sr15/pdf/sr15_spm_final.pdf.

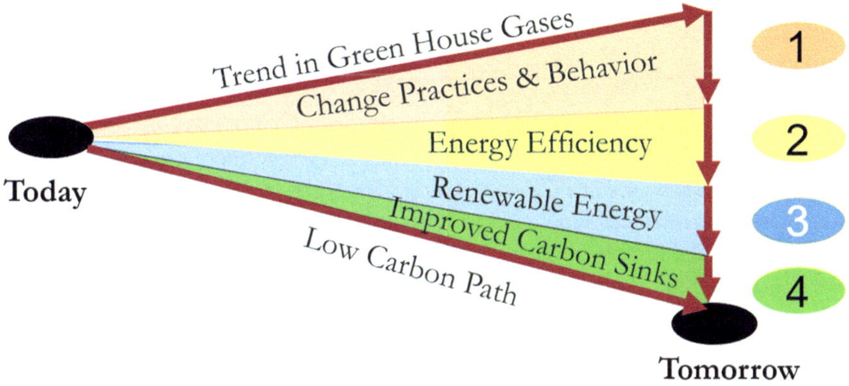

Fig. 1 Key instruments for achieving a low carbon development

and jobs is extremely important, especially as some countries in the Middle East and North Africa (MENA) region have already been struggling with high unemployment for a long time. Moreover, most of the MENA countries if not all of them are rent-seeking economies, with most of the rent is driven and generated by the sale the fossil energy natural resources. On a more complex paradigm, the MENA countries failed to develop a strong industry that takes advantage of the existence of cheap and accessible fossil energy.

In recent years, energy demand in the MENA countries has increased sharply. This trend is mainly due to steady population growth, socio-economic development, and urbanization, driven by both growth-oriented policies and oil and gas revenues.

In recent years, there has been a commitment to stimulating an unprecedented deployment of renewable energy in (MENA) countries. Nevertheless, despite the efforts made and investments in renewable energy, at present, renewable energy sources make a minor contribution to the energy mix, about 0.4%, to the total primary energy in the region (Belaid and Zrelli 2019; Belaïd et al. 2020; Aghahosseini et al. 2020; Omri and Belaïd 2021).

Based on this conjecture, this chapter aims to explore the key challenges and lessons learned in the MENA region regarding the development of renewable energy. First, we briefly review the demand for renewable energy and the resources available, before examining some of the challenges that need to be addressed to meet deployment targets. Second, we discuss the role of Small and Medium-sized Enterprises (SMEs) in driving greed and sustainable inclusive growth in the MENA region.

This chapter will be structured as follows: After an introduction and research background, Sect. 2 provides a brief literature review. Section 3 highlights the potentials and challenges of renewable energy production and challenges in the MENA region, further, this section discusses the situation of some MENA countries and the analysis of their renewable energy policies (Morocco, Lebanon, and Egypt). Section 4 concludes the chapter and provides some policy implications.

2 Literature Review

The investment in renewable energy in the MENA region is a major contributor to setting the region on a path of overall socio-economic and environmental development. The motivation behind increasing renewable energy generation in the MENA region is the improvement of a wide range of sectors in each country's economy. The environmental drivers include limiting pollution by curbing down green-house gas emissions and establishing a secure sustainable source of energy for the region. In terms of economic drivers, the expansion of renewable energy diversifies the economy's sectors will result in the creation of new jobs thus reducing unemployment (Bélaïd et al. 2019; IRENA 2020a, b, c, d, e). A positive economic push is the reduction of technology costs (Smart Energy International 2020).

Renewable energy production capacity installed in the MENA region is approximated to be around 28 GW, 75% of which is hydropower. Nonetheless, renewable energy comprises only 7% of the region's capacity for power generation (Smart Energy International 2020). The most cost-effective and competitive renewable energy resources in the MENA region are solar photovoltaic (PV) and wind energy (Zafar 2020). Energy demand in the MENA region is anticipated to increase steadily at a rate of 1.9% annually (Boyd Anderson 2019). The MENA region has the capacity to expand its renewable energy generation that can comprise 45% of the potential generation for renewable energy in the world (Ramin Jalilvand 2012).

The goals set by governments, in the MENA region, for renewable energy for the next 30 years are ambitious. For example, Dubai's government aims to raise the energy generated from clean sources to 75% of the total energy produced by 2050. The World Future Energy Summit held at the beginning of 2020 in Abu Dhabi confirmed Dubai's new target in massively shifting from unsustainable to sustainable sources of energy (Smart Energy International 2020).

Aghahosseini et al. (2020) investigate whether it is possible for the renewable energy system in the MENA region to constitute 100% of the energy sector by the end of 2030. In the proposed scenario, the Levelized Cost of Energy (LCOE) is estimated to be between 40.3 and 52.8 €/MWh, where the proposed system proves to be 67% on average more affordable than a BAU strategy (Aghahosseini et al. 2020). Future well-being depends on the capacity of the finite resources left for consumption and future generations have, but more importantly on the progress in renewable energy development (Sakmar et al. 2011).

There are several countries in the MENA region that set good examples in the progress towards renewable energy development. Jordan and Egypt have revealed consistent advancement. But Morocco is considered to surpass most other countries in the MENA region, as its government has achieved remarkable progress towards the goal it set: 2 GW for solar PV and 2 GW for wind power by the end of 2020, in accordance with the Nour-1 solar project (Zafar 2020). Moreover, UAE has achieved Dubai's solar park in 2013 and the 100 MW Shams CSP plant is in use since 2014 as well (Zafar 2020). Furthermore, Saudi Arabia's vision for 2030 in the development of renewable energy is promising.

There is no doubt that the MENA region's governments have to overcome a number of challenges, in the transition to more sustainable clean sources of energy. One of the biggest challenges is the reformation of the regulations and the amendment of a wide range of policies. For example, the process of merging photovoltaic solar power into the power grids requires a certain degree of flexibility of the grids, installment of advanced technologies, and setting up well-structured business models. Another challenge is that electricity and water generation are widely linked in the utilities of the MENA region. To successfully expand a system of renewables, this link must be detached (Smart Energy International 2020). In addition, a study revealed that internalizing the externalities (for example, environmental costs like air pollution) that result from using non-renewable energy sources will double the price of electricity for oil and coal (Ramin Jalilvand 2012). Nonetheless, internalizing the negative externalities to be reflected in the cost of electricity of non-renewables is a political obstacle and needs time as well as institutional reform to happen (Ramin Jalilvand 2012).

The governments must increase efficiency in developing renewable energy sources by setting sufficient financial budgets to minimize the LCOE, promoting the infrastructure, and removing fuel subsidies in order to increase incentives to shift toward renewables. There are two types of instruments that the governments can implement to achieve the goals they have set for renewable energy generation: incentivizing renewable energy and disincentivizing non-renewable energy. In other words, subsidizing renewable energy generation instead of non-renewable energy generation is a crucial step that most governments of the MENA region ought to take to move faster on the path of renewable energy development. To incentivize renewable energy, the MENA region governments should pave the way to private organizations to join the renewable energy market by reducing regulative barriers to entry (Abdelrahim 2019). Another tool is price-based subsidies, known as the feed-in tariff would allow access to electricity grids for carriers of renewable energy. Furthermore, a reduction in after-sale tax for producers of renewable energy, easier access to research and development, and lower investment taxes allow producers to earn higher profits thus promoting the expansion and increased generation of renewable energy. To disincentivize non-renewable energy, governments can impose increased tariffs on non-renewable energy and increase investment and sales taxes on non-renewable energy generation (Ramin Jalilvand 2012).

3 Overview of Renewable Energy in the MENA Region: Resources and Potentials

The Middle East and North Africa (MENA) region is considered to be a highly diverse region, with a heterogeneous group of countries, in terms of abundance of distinct resources, trade relations with international countries, technological capabilities, among other features that give each country its unique profile. Compared to the rest of the world, despite the existing wealth of the MENA region in various resources, it is considered still lagging behind the fast progress of renewable energy development. However, there are positive signs that are promising regarding the future of renewable energy expansion in the MENA region, including the availability of technologies and their respective industrial technology providers.

Although the shares of renewable energy are still relatively low compared to countries in other regions, the future of renewable energy seems promising given the optimistic targets set by the various governments in the MENA region. Approximately 80% of non-hydro renewables corresponds to only four countries, making a total of 6% for the renewables out of the total energy generation. But, the fast progress of investment and planning creates optimistic forecasts for the future of renewable energy. For example, across the Arab region, the investment made to renewable energy development increased from USD 1.2 billion in 2008 to USD 11 billion in 2016. According to the established national plans, Variable Renewable Energy (VRE) will contribute to the major part of this development. It's worth mentioning that forecasting international models in local countries is a misleading way of setting targets.

There are several advantages that make the investment in renewable energy a very worthy one. To begin with, the higher is the share of renewable energy of the total energy consumption, the higher proportion of the fuel is saved; this bolsters the countries' energy resources and weakens the risk of facing shortages while meeting the rising demand. Diversifying the energy sources amplifies the energy security and the independence of countries. In addition, renewable energy reduces pollution, particularly greenhouse gas emissions, thus enhancing environmental protection. Besides, this socio-economic growth generates job opportunities and enriches exports.

The key players in the process of renewable energy expansion are ministers, the private sector, transmission system operators (TSOs), utilities, regulators, among other interrelated players. Countries across the MENA region are at different stages in their development process of renewable energy, yet several countries have common concerns. Around six to eight countries in the MENA region are working on orienting the cost projections for the VRE to become better suited to specific corresponding local contexts, by assessing the capacity credits of the VRE of their systems. In addition, some countries are interested in providing flexibility in evaluating the expansion of VRE in terms of costs and progress. Other common concerns include taking action towards the sustainability and stability of the VRE development, seeking improvements in data acquisitions, institution management, and staff training.

Although some targets are common between the countries and many countries welcome cooperation and exchange of plans in developing renewable energy sources, each country still begs specific attention that is best specialized for their respective contexts. Relative to the rest of the MENA countries, Jordan has made good progress regarding the renewable energy development given its relatively high shares of renewable energy infrastructure facilities installed. The National Energy Strategy 2025, which was then amended to 2050 by the National Renewable Energy Action Plan (NREAP) has set a target of 20% for the generated renewable energy out of the total energy generated. Jordan has approximately a current 15.7% of installed renewable energy, targeted to an increase to 20% by 2025, and a current 6.5% of generated renewable energy. Some of the MENA countries have contributed to competitive solar prices. For example, these prices include 17.8 USD/MWh corresponding to the Sakaka project in Saudi Arabia and 29.9 USD/MWh in Dubai (IRENA, MENA 2020a, b, c, d, e). On the other end of the spectrum, Libya and Yemen are examples of the least developed countries in terms of renewable energy in the region.

While the national plans of most of the countries focus on the VRE expansion, Egypt is an exception in the sense that it is more focused on hydro energy which is targeted to an increase of 2.4 GW by 2027. Egypt's current hydro energy is –4.7% and from which the wind energy is –2.3%. In terms of VRE, for the rest of the countries, Algeria has currently 10 MW wind energy produced which is expected to increase to a 23% of the total energy produced by 2030, and 410 MW of solar energy produced, expected to increase to a 62% of the total energy produced by 2030. These targets are very ambitious. As for Bahrain, its solar PV contributed to 5 MW of energy production which is expected to increase to 300 MW by 2035. Iraq's current solar VRE amounts to 37 MW, and the renewable energy target is 5% of generation capacity by 2030. Regarding Lebanon, there are no VRE connected to the grid, but it has a renewable energy share of 1660 MW, out of which 120 MW is from hydro. Renewable energy share is projected to increase to 30% out of the total energy produced by 2030. Morocco has shown significant progress, where a local industry for solar water heaters was built, which is expected to generate 13,000 new jobs. This has further raised expectations of renewable energy development in Morocco, where the target is 53% of Morocco's total installed renewable energy out of total energy generated (IRENA, MENA 2020a, b, c, d, e).

In sum, each country needs a specialized framework with sufficient attention and investment from all its respective interrelated players to fasten the process of renewable energy development. At the same time, encouraging dialogue paves the way towards exchanging country experiences that would provide valuable lessons to all the countries and prevent each country from reinventing the wheel.

3.1 Renewable Energy in Egypt

With oil production of about 588,000 barrels/day, Egypt is the 5th oil producer in Africa. However, with a population of about 98 million, the country is leading the energy consumption in the continent. One of the fastest-growing populations and the economic growth realized in the last years led to a sharp increase in global energy demand. The energy sector is the main driver of the Egyptian socio-economic development, with about 13% of current GDP. According to the 2017 World Bank report, with an electrification rate of about 99.8%, Egypt is near to achieving universal access to electricity. However, the Egyptian electricity Market is characterized by various blackouts and disruption do to some multiple factors, including fuel shortage, the volatility of exported oil prices, sharp population growth, and infrastructure limitations. IRENA reported that, with a peak demand of 28 GW, the Egyptian electricity

Market reached its worst deficit in 2014. The total primary energy supply in Egypt is based, to a large extent, on oil and natural gas (see Fig. 2). In 2014/2015, oil and oil products represented about 50% of the total primary energy supply, and natural gas represented about 45% of total primary energy supply in Egypt. Concerning electricity generation in 2015, about 92% of the electricity was generated from gas and dual-fuel (IRENA 2018).

The total electricity installed capacity was 22,000 MW in 2007, with an expected demand of 74,000 MW in 2030. About 90% of the electricity generation in Egypt is from fossil fuels, mainly by using natural gas (Abdulrahman and Huisingh 2018). In addition, the major energy source (oil and gas) of the country is in continuous depletion. This situation creates major challenges for the country in keeping a continuous and durable energy supply. The growing local energy demand and concern about fossil fuel ongoing depletion, and environmental quality have led Egyptian energy policymakers to think about alternatives to the conventional energy resources use. To achieve these ambitious goals, the Egyptian authorities plan to invest massively in renewable energy sources and to spur the deployment of solar and wind energy across the country. The Egyptian authority's resoluteness to pursue the energy sector diversification is translated into what is called the 2035 Integrated Sustainable Energy Strategy (ISES). This strategy will cost the Egyptian government about 2.5 billion per year until 2030.

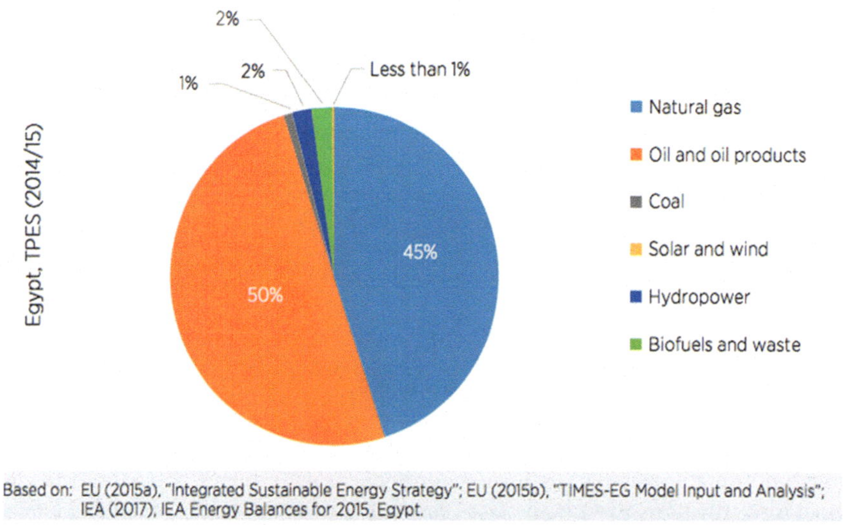

Fig. 2 Egyptian total primary energy supply in 2014/15. *Source* IRENA (2018)

3.1.1 Egyptian Electricity Sector Management

The Egyptian electricity sector is managed by the Ministry of Electricity and Renewable Energy MOERE and supervised by the Supreme Energy Council (SEC). The electricity sector is under the regulation of the Egyptian Electric Utility and Consumer Protection Regulatory Agency, which is in charge of executing policy decisions, setting tariffs, and administering licenses. Historically, generation, transmission, and distribution assets were fully state-owned and operated under the supervision of the Egyptian Electricity Authority (EEA), now known as the EEHC. Transmission, distribution, and generation have been historically under state control via the Egyptian Electricity Authority (EEA), currently known as the Egyptian Electricity Holding Company (EEHC). The private-sector participation started its involvement in the power generation sectors in the late 90s, even though its participation it did not become relevant prior to 2001. The EEHC owns about 90% of electricity generation capacity and the entire state-owned transmission and distribution network. To develop a new competitive power market and end the EEHC on electricity transmission and distribution monopoly, Egyptian authorities introduced in 2015 a new electricity law (No. 87).

3.1.2 Renewable Energy Resources and Potentials

Like other MENA countries, Egypt is richly endowed with renewable energy sources, particularly solar, wind, and biomass. There is a consensus that renewable energy sources represent a viable option for a change in the Egyptian current energy mix, which is still dominated by fossil fuel sources. Increasing the share of renewable energy in Egypt represents a viable solution to address the challenges of the energy sector and improving environmental quality.

Since the late 1970s, the Egyptian authorities have initiated several schemes for testing, demonstrating, and evaluating various renewable energy technology systems and applications in co-operation with several international entities and countries, including Germany, Spain, Italy, Japan, United States, and France. In the last decade, the Egyptian authorities have taken a serious commitment to improving the diversification of energy generation and implementation of energy efficiency measures. Up to now, the renewable energy installed capacity in Egypt around 3.7 gigawatts (GW), in which 2.8 GW is from hydro and 0.887 GW from solar and wind. However, the government aims to generate a supplementary 10 GW from solar and wind power by 2022 (IRENA 2018).

Acknowledging the important role that renewable energy sources could play in addressing this critical situation, the Egyptian authorities created the New and Renewable Energy Authority (NREA) in 1986. In addition to certifications and training programs, the main mission of the NREA was the assessment and promotion of renewable energy in the energy mix through research and development of new technologies. In pursuit of the energy reform agenda, in 2008, the Egyptian Supreme Council of Energy has approved an ambitious strategy and plan to increase the share of renewable sources in the energy mix and reduce the dependency on conventional energy resources. The Egyptian energy diversification strategy is known as the Integrated Sustainable Energy Strategy (ISES) to 2035.

Despite the Egyptian huge solar and wind sources, renewable energy sources are relatively underdeveloped. The renewable energy capacity totalizes 3.7 gigawatts (GW), including 2.8 GW of hydropower and around 0.9 GW of wind and solar power (IRENA 2018). Energy production from renewable sources in Egypt represented about 4% of the global electricity generation in 2009/2010. According to the Egyptian Integrated Energy Strategy plan, the contribution of renewables to energy production in Egypt is predicted to achieve about 8% by 2021/22 and 14% in 2034/35. The evolution of renewable electricity installed capacity for the period 2009–2035 from various renewable sources is displayed in Table 1.

Based on Egypt Vision 2030 scenario, renewable energy is expected to make up 20% and 42% of electricity generation in 2021/22 and 2034/35, respectively. As we can see from the Fig. 3, the average growth rate for renewable energy in the primary energy supply achieves 7.3%.

Table 1 Evolution of renewable energy installed energy capacity for the period 2009–2035 in GW

Type of power station	2009/10	2021/22	2029/30	2034/35
Hydro	2.8	2.8	2.9	2.9
Wind	0.5	13.3	20.6	20.6
PV	0.0	3.0	22.9	31.75
CSP	0.0	0.1	4.1	8.1
Total	3.3	19.2	50.5	62.6

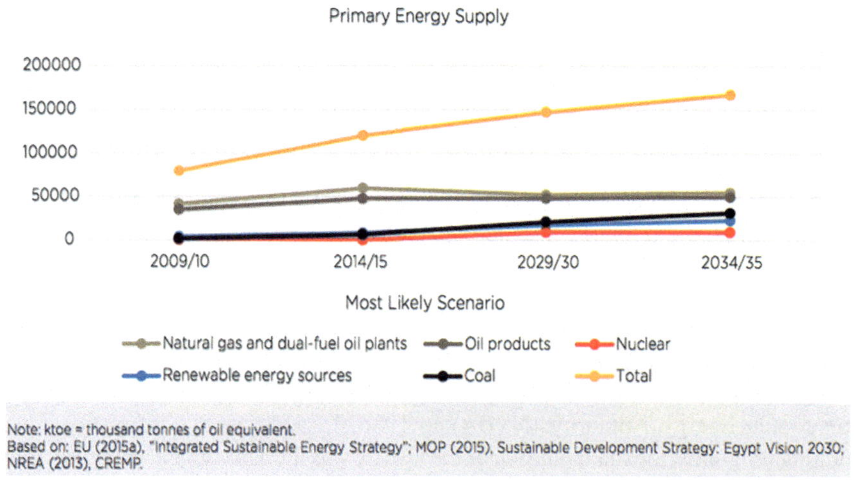

Fig. 3 Primary energy supply (ktoe) in Egypt under the Egyptian Integrated Energy Strategy plan Scenario. *Source* IRENA (2018)

According to this scenario, renewable energy sources, including solar, wind, and hydro, are anticipated to represent about 25% of global installed electricity generation capacity in 2020. Nevertheless, the share of renewable sources in the Egyptian electricity mix is anticipated to reach 42 of the global installed capacity in 2025, following the introduction of nuclear.

3.1.3 Egyptian's Renewable Energy Regulation and Laws

As we stated above, recognizing the role of renewable energy sources in addressing the challenges of the Egyptian energy sector, the Egyptian Ministry of Electricity and Renewable Energy, in line with the Integrated Sustainable Energy Strategy, promulgated a myriad of regulations and laws to accelerate the 2020 and 2035 renewable energy goals implementation. Table 2 displays the key substantial regulations and laws behind the Egyptian energy transition strategy.

Table 2 Overview of the Egyptian energy transition support policies instrument, regulations, and legislation

Regulation	Type
Law No. 102 of the year 1986 establishing the New and Renewable Energy Development and Usage Authority (as amended in 2015)	• Establishes the New and Renewable Energy Authority(NREA) • The NREA has the primary role in promoting and • Developing renewable energy in Egypt
The Constitution of the Arab Republic of Egypt, 2014 (Article 32)	• To gain optimum benefits from renewable energy, promote its investments, and encourage R&D, in addition to local manufacturing
Renewable Energy Law (Decree-Law 203/2014)	• Support the creation of a favorable economic environment for a significant increase in renewable energy investment in the country
Cabinet Decree No. 1947 of the year 2014 on Feed-in Tari	• Establishes the basis for the FIT for electricity produced from renewable energy projects and encourages investment in renewable energy
Prime Ministerial Decree No. (37/4/15/14) of the year 2015	• Regulations to avail land for renewable energy projects
New Electricity Law No. 87 of 2015	• To provide legislative and regulatory frameworks needed to realize the electricity market reform targets
Investment Law No. 72 of the year 2017	• Ensures investment guarantees and amendments as of May 2017 • Establishes a new arbitration center for settling disputes • Codifies social responsibility • Instigates foreign investment in Egypt

Source IRENA (2018)

3.1.4 Egyptian Renewable Energy Potential

Hydropower energy

Up to now, the hydropower is the most mature renewable energy technologies in Egypt. The renewable energy generated from hydropower plants record and average growth of 1.2% per year during the period 2011/2016. Up to now, various hydroelectric stations have been realized. The detail of the hydroelectric capacity and their annual generated electricity in 2015 displayed in Table 3.

Wind energy

Egypt has a huge potential for wind energy resources, notably in the Gulf of Suez. Thanks to its constant wind speed, this region has one of the best locations for mobilizing wind energy in the world. Hurghada station was the first wind farm realized in Egypt in 1993, with a total capacity of 5.2 MW. A number of large-scale wind farms have been realized since that, with a global capacity of 545 M. Table 4 displays information about the Egyptian designed wind farms project until 2023.

Solar energy

Egypt is endowed with high and favorable solar intensity. According to the solar atlas for Egypt, the annual sunshine range between 2900–3200 h, with a direct energy density as 1970–3200 kW h/m^2 per year. The technical electricity-generating potential from solar is about 73.6 Petawatt (pWh) (Aliyu et al. 2018). According to the IRENA report (IRENA 2018), Egypt has one of the most viable regions worldwide for harnessing solar power. Egyptian installed power capacity of small-scale PV totalized about 6 MW in 2013, whereas about 30 MW of off-grid power capacity was installed at the end of 2016. The New and Renewable Energy Authority achieved feasibilities studies for two large-scale PV projects with a generation capacity of 20 MW and 26 MW, respectively. These two plants are expected to be operational in late 2019, with an expected annual production of about 32 GWh and 42 GWh, respectively. Table 5 provides further information on the planned PV project in Egypt up to 2023.

Table 3 Egyptian hydroelectric stations capacity and their annual generated electricity in 2015

Station	Capacity (MW)	Annual generated electricity (GW)
High dam	2100	9484
Aswan 1	280	1578
Aswan 2	270	1523
Esna	86	507
Naga Hamady	64	453
Total	2800	13,545

Table 4 Planned wind farms projects in Egypt until 2023

Project	Technology	Status	Size (MW)	Contract
Gulf of Suez	Wind	Under development	250	NREA-KfW, EIB, AFD EPC scheme
Gulf of Suez	Wind	Under development	250	GDF Suez, Toyota, Orascom BOO scheme
Gulf of Suez	Wind	Under development	200	NREA-Masdar EPC scheme
Gulf of Suez	Wind	Under development	200	AFD-KfW EPC scheme
Gulf of Suez	Wind	Under development	2000	Siemens EPC scheme
Gabal El Zayt	Wind	Under construction	220	NREA-Japan-JICA EPC scheme
Gulf El Zayt	Wind	Under construction	320	Italgen BOO scheme
Gabal El Zayt	Wind	Under construction	120	Spain-NREA
West Nile-1	Wind	Under development	250	BOO scheme
West Nile	Wind	Under development	200	Japan EPC scheme
West Nile	Wind	Tender-bidding Phase	600	NREA IPP scheme

Notes AFD Agence Française de Développement; *EIB* European Investment Bank; *JICA* Japan International Cooperation Agency. Based on: EEHC (2016a), Egyptian Electricity Holding Company Annual Report 2015/16; EU (2015a), "Integrated Sustainable Energy Strategy"; Eversheds and PricewaterhouseCoopers (2016), Developing Renewable Energy Projects: A Guide to Achieving Success in the Middle East, Fourth Edition; MOERE (2017), Full Scale Program for Renewable Energy in Egypt

Table 5 Planned PV projects in egypt until 2023

Project	Type	Status	Size (MW)	Contract
Kom Ombo	PV	Binding	200	BOO scheme
West Nile	PV	Binding	600	Sky Power and EETC BOO
West Nile	PV	Binding	200	EETC BOO
West Nile	PV	Binding	600	BOO scheme
FIT	PV	Operational	50	EETC PPA
FIT	PV	Under development	1415	EETC PPA
Hurghada	PV	Tendering	20	NREA-JICA EPC scheme
Zaafarana	PV	Under development	50	NREA-AFD EPC scheme
Kom Ombo	PV	Under development	26	NREA-AFD EPC scheme
Kom Ombo	PV	Under development	50	NREA-AFD EPC scheme

Note BOO build, own, operate; *EETC* Egyptian Electricity Transmission Co.; *PPA* power purchase agreement; *NREA* New and Renewable Energy Authority (Egypt); *JICA* Japan International Cooperation Agency; *EPC* engineering, procurement and construction; *AFD* French Development Agency (Agence Française de Développement)

3.2 Renewable Energy in Morocco

In 2015, the Moroccan government officially committed itself to the UN's Sustainable Development Goals (SDG), which aims to further reduce poverty and inequality by 2030, thus achieving sustainable, inclusive economic growth as well as promoting social cohesion and innovation. The "Stratégie Nationale de Développement Durable 2030" (SNDD), published by the government in 2017, is based on a national consultation process that was developed in collaboration with relevant international actors. Among others, the strategy describes how the SDGs should be taken into consideration in national planning and budgeting processes. Progress in achieving the SDGs is reviewed by the Haut Commissariat au Plan in cooperation with international actors. The 2009 national energy strategy defined a target of 42% of the total installed capacity to come from renewable energy sources by 2020. This led to the commissioning of new plants to increase the total capacity to 2000 MW of solar, 2000 MW of wind, and 2000 MW of hydropower by 2020 (IEA 2020).

In 2015, at the 21st session of the Conference of the Parties to the UNFCCC (COP21), Morocco announced a further planned increase in renewable energy capacity to reach 52% of the total by 2030 (20% solar, 20% wind, 12% hydropower). To reach the 2030 target, the country aims to add about 10 GW of renewable energy capacity between 2018 and 2030, for example, 4560 MW of solar capacity, 4200 MW of wind capacity, and 1330 MW of hydroelectric capacity (IEA 2020). In accordance with these plans, there are currently several projects organized and being executed for solar and wind energy.

Solar energy project in Morocco

Following the Moroccan's renewable energy plan, there are currently several solar projects planned and being executed as well as the locations of construction are selected under criteria of highest solar irradiance (see Table 6).

One drawback is that the biggest agglomerations are North-West, whereas the strongest irradiation is found South-East. It needs to be mentioned that despite ambitious renewable energy plans back in 2017, two new thermal powerplants were finished (Centrale thermique de Safi and Jerada/ Thermal Power Station with a total

Table 6 Solar power plants specifiactions in Mrocco

Location	Capacity (MW)	dni (kwh/m^2/year)	Area (ha)	Planned commissioning
Ouarzazate	500	2635	2500	2015
Ain Ben Mathar	400	2290	2000	2017
Boujdour	100	2628	500	2020
Sebkhat Tah/Tarfaya	500	2140	2500	2019
Foum Al Ouad/Laayoune	500	2628	2500	2019

capacity of over 1800 MW). In comparison to the energy output of one of the flagship renewable power stations, the NOOR project merely produces 500–580 MW in the final stage. Nor is an ambitious solar power plant that is under construction and of which three phases have already been completed (Fig. 4).

Looking more closely at the business model from an economic point of view, the solar electricity production in the Moroccan desert is internationally not competitive as it is more expensive than electricity generated in conventional gas and coal-fired power plants. At an average of 12 Euro cents/kWh, the production costs will not be competitive and have to be subsidized by the state economic efficiency, as well as the environmental impact, have to be carefully considered as in order to operate the thermal storage which needs to maintain a minimum temperature of above 100 degrees. Back-up fuel is needed for the Ouarzazate complex, estimated to be at 19t/day of gasoil for a capacity of 500 MW (African Development Bank Group 2020)

Additionally, the preferred geographic location for the highest solar irradiance efficiency in the atlas implies that it is far away from the big coastal agglomerations (as can be seen in the table above). This introduces two further inefficiency factors: Electric power transmission and distribution losses. This describes the losses in transmission between sources of supply and points of distribution in Morocco, where

Fig. 4 Wind and solar power stations in Morocco. *Source* The Wind Power (2020)

the average loss was 14.7% of the input. This is of concern, as the biggest central town is Marrakesh (100 km distance) and the other agglomerations are costal.

Wind power in morocco

Table 7 beneath shows the increase in wind energy generation capacity in Morocco.

Besides the already installed capacity, further projects are underway in order to reach the objective of 2000 MW in 2020 (Table 8).

Furthermore, the cost construction, as well as the cost of storage, must be included in the wind power systems in order to meet peak demand. This is mostly done by pumped-storage hydroelectricity. This is an important extra cost that needs to be attributed to the cost of wind power. Besides storage expanding, the network is also a possibility to increase the price efficiency as it means attaining access to new markets. Therefore, Morocco is currently planning to build a third link with Spain. The Spanish government revealed that the new electricity link is designed to promote green energy trading. This agreement will have a strong focus on renewable energy and energy efficiency, in addition to grid integration and by linking regional energy markets. All these elements would favor the renewable energy plan in Morocco. The Moroccan initiative proposed increasing the capacity of the existing interconnections with Spain by 700 MW. Furthermore, Spain and Morocco contemplated building a new 600-MW electric interconnection including Portugal. This would increase the commercial interconnection capacity between Spain and Portugal as well. This option, however, could not be worked out during the negotiations. (Morocco Energy Situation—energypedia.info 2020).

Table 7 Wind energy projects in Morocco

Year	Capacity (MW)	Growth (MW)	Growth %
1998	0	0	–
2000	54	40	285.8
2002	54	0	–
2004	54	0	–
2006	64	0	–
2008	125	0	–
2010	286	33	13.1
2012	291	0	–
2013	495	204	70.2
2014	787	292	59
2015	787	0	–
2016	787	0	–
2017	787	0	–
2018	907	120	15.3
2019	1200	293	32.4

Source The Wind Power (2020)

Table 8 Ongoing wind energy projects

City	Capacity (MW)
Tanger1	140
Tanger2	150
Khallada	120
Haouma	50
Koudia Baida	300
Khallada	120
Taza	150
Midelt	100
Taza	100
Jbel Hdid	200
Akfenir	200
Tarfaya	300
Tiskrad	300
Boujdour	100
Laayoune	50
Amougdoul	60

Source The Wind Power (2020)

3.3 Renewable Energy in Lebanon

Lebanon, the green country at the heart of the Mediterranean, is fortunate with its natural resources and abundance of water, wind, and sun. While citizens enjoy the natural beauty of the country, serious problems like the unsolved problem of electricity cuts leave Lebanon's renewable energy yet far from being well-invested. The year 1970 has marked a new era for renewable energy in Lebanon. Before then, 75% of the produced electricity relied on biomass heating. The development of the renewable energy sector in recent decades has been mostly in the power sector, despite the crucial role that all the sectors play in energy generation. According to the Ministry of Energy and Water in Lebanon, there are around 5 hydroelectric power stations that have been installed between 1931 and 1967, which corresponds to an installed capacity of 286 MW (Ministry of Energy and Water, Lebanon 2019).

In 2010, the electricity reform paper introduced renewable energy foundations. It was then stretched in Lebanon's first National Energy Efficiency Action Plan (NEEAP). The renewable energy targets took their share in the Nationally Determined Contribution (NDC) to the Paris Agreement. The Lebanese government has set several targets on renewable energy as a fraction of electricity consumption, which prior to 2018, was an initial 12% of the total electricity and heating by 2020, increased in 2018 to a target of 30% by 2030. In 2020, the target of renewable energy has been amended to 20% out of electricity and heating, 15% out of which is unconditional and 5% is conditional. This would be considered significant progress compared to a share of renewable energy consumption that amounted to less than 1% in 2014.

As a result of the targets set since 2018, the National Energy Efficiency and Renewable Energy Action (NEEREA) was initiated with the support of the Central Bank of Lebanon (BDL) by lowering the interest rates on the renewable energy projects, providing for each project a loan with a maximum of USD 10 million and an upper period of 14 years to be paid back. In addition, in 2018, Lebanon signed its first power purchase agreement (PPA) for renewable energy consumption which held a total capacity of 226 MW.

Renewable energy forms in Lebanon include hydropower, onshore wind, and solar power. The first form of renewable energy, which has four corresponding sources: reconstruction of existing power plants that would be expected to contribute to an increase of an annual 1000 GMh in energy consumption, a corresponding 358 MW building new ones, 263 MW hydroelectric energy from river flowing water (Sogreah-Artelia 2012), and lastly around 5 MW for non-river energy sources. As for onshore wind, Gharrad Hassan in his publication "The national wind atlas for Lebanon", provided the first mean wind estimation in 2011, which had a potential capacity of 6100 MW (Garrad Hassan 2011). According to the National Renewable Energy Action Plan (NREAP), the targets for the wind energy capacity amounted to 200 MW by 2020 and 45 MW by 2030. The third form of renewable energy which is solar power. The installed capacity of distributed solar photovoltaic solar systems has developed from 1 MPp in 2012 to 56 MWp in 2018 (DREG 2017). Large-scale solar power plants are targeted at 300 MWp by 2030.

The development of renewable energy will require prolonged investment and attention from policymakers to meet the ongoing demands and the arising concerns with the recent pandemic Covid-19. Renewable energy expansion will necessitate more sustainable regulations, better scalable measures, promotion of technology, installment of tools for energy generation from heating and cooling, bolster banking regulation that promotes energy investments, and enhancing the role of private sector financing.

4 Conclusions and Policy Implications

Centuries of dependence on fossil fuels have led to severe environmental damage and centralized generation, distribution, and power structures from which only a few countries benefit. The hunger for energy of a growing population is becoming ever greater and promotes new, extreme forms of energy production. The new needs regarding supply security cannot any longer be satisfied with conventional energy sources. Consequently, it is becoming increasingly problematic to achieve the security of supply, ecological sustainability energy justice, and economic stability. Energy transformation should be part of a fundamental paradigm shift towards a sustainable development model.

MENA countries have one of the greatest renewable energy potentials in the world, and will probably be the most vulnerable to the horrific effects of climate change. Unfortunately, only a few countries have exploited this potential, as non-renewable energy still dominates the total energy mix in most countries. Many pieces of evidence show that investments in energy transition can boost GDP and create jobs (IRENA 2020a, b, c, d, e). In addition, national and regional energy transitions can help build resilient economies and societies. Therefore, linking short-term actions to medium- and long-term strategies is vital to achieving the Paris agreement on climate change the Sustainable Development Goals (SDGs).

There is a consensus among economists that moving away from proven fossil fuel-based development paths requires costly additional investments in the energy system (Leimbach et al. 2018). Moreover, MENA economies are rent seeking-based economies that rely heavily on the declining petro-Dollar rent generated. The shift towards RE business model would imply abandoning wasting, and heavily subsidizing fossil non-renewable energy sources. The shift implies a full economic transformation rather than just an energy transition. Nonetheless, the large potential for renewable energy in the MENA region, especially solar energy, and the international diffusion of technologies could facilitate the transformation to a low-carbon economy and thus the adoption of emission reduction commitments (Belaid and Youssef 2017; Amri et al. 2018; Belaid et al. 2019). The main purpose of this Chapter is to explore the role of renewable energy in shaping energy transition. The setting of the analysis is the MENA region, as examples of growing economies, most of them experiencing extensive economic and energy reforms. Renewable energy is rapidly gaining relevance as the main technology to stifle the increasing demand for energy on the MENA countries, and most of the MENA governments initiated energy renewable energy legislation.

To summarize, aggressive RE policies are vital to achieving key energy-policy goals, and the so-called “multiple benefits” of RE in the MENA region, such as addressing climate change and air pollution, improving energy security, and increasing energy access. Policies should be more ambitious to address national challenges and targets and strengthen climate commitments. Linking short-term actions to medium- and long-term strategies are vital to achieving the Paris agreement on climate change the Sustainable Development Goals (SDGs). However, securing strategic financing, diverting investment from fossil fuels, investing in transition-related infrastructures, and making bailouts conditional on climate action should be a cornerstone of national strategies.

References

Abdelrahim F (2019) The rise of renewable energy in the MENA region: an investigation into the policies governing energy resources. University of Pennsylvania Scholarly Commons. Available at: https://web.archive.org

Abdulrahman AO, Huisingh D (2018) The role of biomass as a cleaner energy source in Egypt's energy mix. J Clean Prod 172:3918–3930

African Development Bank Group (2020) African development bank group. Available at: https://www.afdb.org/fileadmin/uploads/afdb/Documents/Environmental-and-Social-Assessments/MoroccoMorocco_-_Ouarzazate_Solar_Power_Station_Project_II_-_ESIA_Summary.pdf

Aghahosseini A, Bogdanov D, Breyer C (2020) Towards sustainable development in the MENA region: Analysing the feasibility of a 100% renewable electricity system in 2030. Energy Strategy Rev 28:100466. https://doi.org/10.1016/j.esr.2020.100466

Aliyu AK, Modu B, Tan CW (2018) A review of renewable energy development in Africa: a focus in South Africa, Egypt, and Nigeria. Renew Sustain Energy Rev 81:2502–2518

Amri F, Bélaïd F, Roubaud D (2018) Does technological innovation improve environmental sustainability in developing countries? Some evidence from tunisia. J Energy Dev 44(1/2):41–60

Artelia S (2012) Schema directeur hydro-electrique du liban. Ministry of Energy and Water, Beirut

Belaid F, Youssef M (2017) Environmental degradation, renewable and non-renewable electricity consumption, and economic growth: Assessing the evidence from Algeria. Energy Policy 102:277–287

Belaid F, Zrelli MH (2019) Renewable and non-renewable electricity consumption, environmental degradation and economic development: evidence from Mediterranean countries. Energy Policy 133:110929

Belaid F, Elsayed AH, Belaid F (2019) What drives renewable energy production in MENA Region? Investigating the roles of political stability, governance and financial sector. Econ Res Forum Working Pap (No. 1322)

Belaïd F, Ben Youssef A, Omri A, Yusuf Al-Hamad M, Alabbasi AI (2019) South-south ideas—renewable energy in the Middle East and North Africa Region—potential and limits. United Nations Office for South-South Cooperation and the United Nations Development Programme

Belaïd F, Boubaker S, Kafrouni R (2020) Carbon emissions, income inequality and environmental degradation: the case of Mediterranean countries. Eur J Comp Econ 17(1):73–102

Bélaïd F, Ben Youssef A, Omri A, Al-Hamad MY, Alabbasi AI (2019) South-south ideas—renewable energy in the Middle East and North Africa region—potential and limits. United Nations

Boyd Anderson K (2019) Renewable energy on the rise in the Middle East, Arab News. Available at: https://www.arabnews.com/node/1448021

BP (2017) Statistical review of world energy. British Petroleum

DREG (Small Decentralized Renewable Energy Power Generation Project) (2017) 2017 Solar PV status report for Lebanon. UNDP, Beirut

Electricité du Liban (EDL). http://www.edl.gov.lb/

Gebran B (2010) Policy paper for the electricity sector. Ministry of Energy and Water, Beirut

Hassan G (2011) The national wind atlas for Lebanon. UNDP-CEDRO, Beirut

IEA (2020) Morocco renewable energy target 2030. Policies, IEA

IRENA (2017) Renewable energy auctions: analysing 2016. International Renewable Energy Agency, Abu Dhabi

IRENA (2018) Renewable energy outlook: egypt. International Renewable Energy Agency, Abu Dhabi

IRENA (2019a) Renewable power generation costs in 2018. International Renewable Energy Agency, Abu Dhabi

IRENA (2019b) Renewable energy in Lebanon: can the country embrace its resources sustainably?, Heinrich-Böll-Stiftung. Available at: https://lb.boell.org/en/2019/03/01/renewable-energy-lebanon-can-country-embrace-its-resources-sustainably

IRENA (2020a) Global renewables outlook. International Renewable Energy Agency, Abu Dhabi

IRENA (2020b) Power sector planning in arab countries: incorporating variable renewables. International Renewable Energy Agency, Abu Dhabi

IRENA (2020c) Renewable energy outlook: Lebanon. International Renewable Energy Agency, Abu Dhabi

IRENA (2020d) Middle East and North Africa. IRENA. Available at: https://www.irena.org/mena
IRENA (2020e) Middle East and North Africa. IRENA. https://www.irena.org/mena
Lebanese Center for Energy Conservation (2019) The evolution of the solar water heaters market in lebanon
Leimbach M, Roming N, Schultes A, Schwerhoff G (2018) Long-term development perspectives of Sub-Saharan Africa under climate policies. Ecol Econ 144:148–159
Mongo M, Belaïd F, Ramdani B (2021) The effects of environmental innovations on CO2 emissions: Empirical evidence from Europe. Environ Sci Policy 118:1–9
Ministry of Energy and Water (2019) Announcement by the Lebanese Ministry of Energy and Water (MEW) at the international beirut energy forum 2019. Beirut
Omri A, Belaïd F (2021) Does renewable energy modulate the negative effect of environmental issues on the socio-economic welfare? J Environ Manag 278:111483
Ramin Jalilvand D (2012) Renewable energy for the Middle East and North Africa policies for a successful transition. Friedrich Ebert Stiftung (FES). Available at: https://web.archive.org
Sakmar SL et al (2011) Sustainable development and environmental challenges in the mena region: Accounting for the environment in the 21st century'. Economic Research Forum. Available at: https://web.archive.org
Smart Energy International (2020) MENA commits to renewable energy despite new challenges. Available at: https://www.smart-energy.com/renewable-energy/mena-commits-to-renewable-energy-despite-new-challenges/
The Wind Power (2020) *Morocco—Map—Countries—Online Access—The Wind Power*. [online] Thewindpower.net. Available at: https://www.thewindpower.net/country_maps_en_28_morocco.php. Accessed 26 July 2020
Tiba S, Belaid F (2020) The pollution concern in the era of globalization: Do the contribution of foreign direct investment and trade openness matter? Energy Econ 104966
Tiba S, Belaid F (2021) Modeling the nexus between sustainable development and renewable energy: The african perspectives. J Econ Surv 35(1):307–329.
Zafar S (2020) Renewables market in MENA. BioEnergy Consult. Available at: https://www.bioenergyconsult.com/renewables-market-mena/#:~:text=MENA%20region%20has%20an%20attractive,billion%20per%20year%20by%202020

Fateh Belaid is a Full Professor of Economics at the Lille Catholic University, Director of the Smart & Sustainable Cities research unit, with appointments in Ecole des Ponts & Chaussées ParisTech, and Ecole Nationale des Sciences Géographiques. He is also a Research Fellow at the Economic Research Forum. He received an HDR (Habilitation for Supervising Doctoral Research) from Orléans University, a Ph.D. in Economics and an M.S. degree in Applied Economics & Decision Theory from Littoral Côte d'Opale University, as well as M.S. degrees in Statistics from the National Institute of Statistics and Applied Economics. He is an energy and environmental economist drawing from the fields of applied microeconomics, energy modeling, and econometrics. Dr. Belaïd is already recognized as a productive scholar in a number of fields, the focal point being environmental and energy economics but also in energy policy, decision-making process, and time series econometrics. He has published widely on household energy consumption, energy-saving behaviours, individual preference and investment in energy efficiency, fuel poverty, as well as on renewable energy and energy policy. Outlets for his work have included Ecological Economics, Energy Economics, Journal of Economic Surveys, Journal of Environmental Management, Energy Policy, Structural Changes and Economic Dynamics, Journal of Environmental Science & Policy; Finance Research Letters, Applied Economics Letters; European Journal of Comparative Economics, The Journal of Energy and Development, and Renewable & Sustainable Energy Reviews.

Elias Boukrami is the Head of Programmes' portfolio of Finance, Energy and Trade. His portfolio of programmes includes the M.Sc. Oil and Gas Trade Management a programme that he led during creation and successful development in 2014. More recently he led a team academic and professionals that validated the new MSc Finance and Investment with four specialism pathways, including Banking/Fintech, Wealth Management, Energy Trade and Financial Trading. His team under his leadership was awarded the 2014 Trustees' Prize for Outstanding Service to Regents University London. Dr. Boukrami is the associate director of the Regent's Transnational Centre for Business and Management. Dr. Boukrami is a Fellow member of the Higher Education Academy, a member of Energy Institute, a member of the Westminster Energy Forum and member of the Chartered Management Institute. Dr. Boukrami holds a Ph.D. in Empirical Finance where his area of research was financial derivatives and particularly swaps. His current research is the "Business Models Innovation" arena; he is interested in the causal effects of innovation on business models dynamics, particularly in the financial services sector.

Razan Amine is a Research Assistant at The Johns Hopkins University—Paul H. Nitze School of Advanced International Studies (SAIS). She received a Master of International Economics and Finance (MIEF) From Johns Hopkins University.

Oil Price and Electricity Firms: Robust Evidence from the U.S. Economy During the COVID-19 Era

Hela Mzoughi and Amine Ben Amar

Abstract This study investigates volatility spillover effects among oil prices and a set of major and minor U.S. electricity corporations' stock prices from 1st January 2019 to 31 August 2020. Based on the Diebold and Yilmaz's (2012) spillover measure, our results show that, whether before or during COVID-19 pandemic, volatility spillovers of the U.S. electricity market tend to be grouped according to company size in terms of market capitalization. The oil market seems to be a net volatility receiver and its sensitivity to the electricity companies' volatilities is even more important during the COVID-19 crisis period.

1 Introduction

According to the IEA oil market report (2020) and the World Bank commodity markets outlook (2020), the COVID-19 pandemic represents an unprecedented negative demand shock to oil markets and to global energy-related sectors. Indeed, with the onset of the corona virus pandemic in early 2020, oil prices fell dramatically. The catalyst for the initial decline in oil prices is attributed to the Russia-OPEC price war in March 2020, leading ultimately Saudi Arabia to flood the oil market. Adding to that, on April 20, as WTI neared its expiration date for delivery in May, the lack of available storage capacity caused a wave of panic among traders holding derivative contracts that collapsed and found it impossible to resell them. It was a particular situation that made the crude stream (WTI) traded at Cushing–Oklahoma, the benchmark for U.S. oil, fell as low as minus $37 a barrel; the cost of Brent also dropped, but not as much. In addition, this volatile behavior of oil prices resulted in a spillover impact on oil-dependent sectors such as electricity sector (Figueroa et al. 2020; IEA,

H. Mzoughi (✉)
University of Tunis Carthage-Carthage Business School, ESMA-Higher School of Statistics and Information Analysis, Tunis, Tunisia
e-mail: hela.mzoughi@utctunisie.com

A. B. Amar
International University of Rabat, RBS College of Management, Rabat, Morocco
e-mail: amine.ben-amar@uir.ac.ma

S. Goutte et al. (eds.), *Advances in Managing Energy and Climate Risks*, Lecture Notes in Energy 82, https://doi.org/10.1007/978-3-030-71403-1_2

2020). Indeed, the ongoing worldwide COVID-19 pandemic caused a collapse in electricity demand and impacted future forecasting (Abu-Rayash and Dincer 2020). The effects of social distancing guidelines affect U.S. electricity consumption: many businesses cut back production or have closed and many people are working from home. Hence, there is a significant increase in residential load demand while there is a substantial decrease in commercial and industrial loads.

The literature dealing with the impact of COVID-19 pandemic on energy market, in connection with the exceptional drop in oil demand with various assets, is expanding. Within commodities market, Gharib et al. (2020), Dutta et al. (2020) and Mensi et al. (2020) from others, try to assess the impact of the ongoing pandemic on the relationship between oil and gold using different techniques. Salisu et al. (2020) and Sharif et al. (2020), among others, highlight the oil-stocks behavior nexus during the pandemic. Wang et al. (2020) explore the impact of COVID-19 on the cross-correlations between crude oil and agri-cultural futures markets. Also, from an environmental perspective, Mzoughi et al. (2020) focuses on the impact of the COVID-19 pandemic on the connection between oil and CO_2 emissions. However, very few empirical studies analyze the impact of the COVID-19 pandemic on the interdependence between oil prices and the electricity market. For instance, Norouzi and Fani (2020), Norouzi et al. (2020) point out the ongoing pandemic effects on the oil and electricity demand in China. Moreover, recent studies examine the interdependence between oil prices and stock markets using aggregate and firm-level data (Sadorsky 2012; Antonakakis et al. 2018; Ben Amar et al. 2020), nevertheless, to the best of our knowledge, no studies have explored the volatility spillover effects in U.S. energy markets during the ongoing pandemic.

To fill this gap, this paper contributes to the existing literature dealing with the impact of the COVID-19 pandemic on energy markets by examining volatility spillovers between oil prices and the U.S. electricity corporations' stock prices over the period from January 1st, 2019 to August 31st, 2020. To the best of our knowledge, our is the first empirical study that investigates volatility spillovers among oil prices and electricity corporation stock prices by using the Diebold and Yilmaz's (2012) spillover index framework. Results suggest that total volatility spillovers index is relatively higher during the COVID-19 crisis, and that spillovers effects seem to be grouped according to electricity company's size.

The remainder of the paper is as follow. Section 2 introduces the empirical strategy and the data. Section 3 discusses the results. Section 4 concludes.

2 Empirical Strategy and Data

2.1 Empirical Strategy

To examine the spillovers in returns among oil prices and a set of major and minor electricity corporations' stock prices during the period between the 1st January 2019 to 31th August 2020, we use the Diebold and Yilmaz's (2012) spillover measure which is based on VAR forecast error variance decompositions. Diebold and Yilmaz (2012) consider a VAR(q), $\upsilon_t = \zeta_0 + \sum_{i=1}^{q} \zeta_i \upsilon_{t-i} + \varepsilon_t$, where $\upsilon_t^{'}$ is the vector of size M of endogenous variables; ζ_i are $M \times M$ parameter matrices and $\varepsilon \sim (0, \Gamma)$ is a $M \times 1$ vector of *iid* disturbances. The moving-average representation of this process is $\upsilon_t = \zeta_0 + \sum_{i=0}^{\infty} B_i \varepsilon_{t-i}$, where the $M \times M$ coefficient matrices B_i obey $B_i = \zeta_1 B_{i-1} + \zeta_2 B_{i-2} + \ldots + \zeta_p B_{i-p}$, with B_0 an $M \times M$ identity matrix and with $B_i = 0$ for $i < 0$. Since computation of the variance decompositions requires innovations orthogonalization, external coefficient restrictions are required to estimate the coefficient matrix B_i. While the Cholesky decomposition of the covariance matrix allows to achieve orthogonality, this identification scheme makes the variance decompositions sensitive to the ordering of the variables in the vector of endogenous variables. To address this problem and produce impulse responses that are insensitive to the order of variables, Diebold and Yilmaz (2012) used the generalized VAR framework of Koop et al. (1996) and Pesaran and Shin (1998). The generalized impulse response function is defined by $B_j^G(i) = \sqrt{\sigma_{jj}} B_i \Gamma u_j$, where $\sqrt{\sigma_{jj}}$ is the standard deviation of the error term for the jth equation and u_j is a $M \times 1$ selection vector. Pesaran and Shin (1998) demonstrate that the N-step-ahead forecast error variance decompositions, $F_{ij}^G(N)$, is given by

$$F_{ij}^G(N) = \frac{\sigma_{jj}^{-1} \sum_{n=0}^{N-1} \left(u_i^{'} B_n \Gamma u_j\right)^2}{\sum_{n=0}^{N-1} \left(u_i^{'} B_n \Gamma B_n^{'} u_i\right)}, \quad i, j = 1, \ldots, M \tag{1}$$

Yilmaz (2012) define a spillover measure, $\mathfrak{S}_{DY}^G$, as

$$\mathfrak{S}_{DY}^G = \frac{\sum_{i,j=1, i \neq j}^{M} \tilde{F}_{ij}^G(N)}{M} \cdot 100 \quad \text{with } \tilde{F}_{ij}^G(N) = \frac{F_{ij}^G(N)}{\sum_{j=1}^{M} F_{ij}^G(N)} \tag{2}$$

The spillover index, $\mathfrak{S}_{DY}^G$, measures the contribution of spillovers of volatility shocks to variable $j = 1, \ldots, M$ to the total forecast error variance of variable $i = 1, \ldots, M$, with $i \neq j$.

2.2 Data

Our underlying data are daily observations of the crude oil Brent US$/BBL (**OIL**) and the stock prices of a panel of the five highest and the five lowest NYSE electricity companies' capitalizations. All series are expressed in U.S. dollars. Data are collected from Datastream database and cover the period running from January 1st, 2019 to August 31st, 2020, a total of 435 observations. The selected electricity companies are the following: Nextera Energy (**NXT$_{\mathbf{H}}$**), Dominion Energy (**DOM$_{\mathbf{H}}$**), Southern (**STH$_{\mathbf{H}}$**), american electric power (**AEP$_{\mathbf{H}}$**), Eversource Energy (**EVR$_{\mathbf{H}}$**), Tennessee Valley Authority (**TVA$_{\mathbf{L}}$**), Unitil (**UNT$_{\mathbf{L}}$**), Kenon Holdings (**KNH$_{\mathbf{L}}$**), Azure Power Global (**APG$_{\mathbf{L}}$**), Bloom Energy (**BLM$_{\mathbf{L}}$**). **H** and **L** in subscript refer to highest and lowest capitalization, respectively. Stock returns are calculated as the daily change in the log of the stock prices, *i.e.* $y_t = \log(P_t) - \log(P_{t-1})$, and standardized, *i.e.* $v_t = (y_t - \mathbb{E}(y_t))/\sigma(y_t)$. Daily returns are presented in Fig. 1.

Although the visual inspection from Fig. 1 shows that OIL and electricity firms' returns share some common return peaks, we notice that the returns of the firms with the largest capitalizations behave more homogeneously. Another observation worth mentioning here is the relative higher volatility exhibited by firms with the lowest capitalizations compared to those with the largest capitalizations. Table 1 provides descriptive statistics for stock returns.

3 Empirical Results

In this section, we investigate the volatility spillovers among oil prices and stock prices using firm-level data of electricity corporations. Tables 2, 3 and 4 report the static spillover analysis for the entire sample period (Table 2), the pre-COVID-19 period (Table 3) and the COVID-19 period (Table 3). Their (*i, j*)-th elements are the estimated contributions to the forecast error variance components of stock *i* coming from an innovation in stock *j*. The static total spillover index, reported in the south-east corner of each table, is the off-diagonal row sum relative to the row sum including diagonals, expressed as a percentage. We notice that the static total volatility spillover index is relatively higher during the COVID-19 period (58.3%) than during the pre-COVID-19 period (41%), indicating a relatively greater interdependence among volatilities during the COVID-19 crisis.

Results presented in Tables 2, 3 and 4 suggest that return spillovers to others from each of the considered corporations' stock prices tend to be grouped according to company size, *i.e.* that they differ considerably depending on whether the company belongs to the highest or lowest capitalizations. Indeed, companies with high capitalization are rather influenced by other companies having high capitalization, while companies with low capitalization are influenced by other companies having low capitalization, except for UNITIL corporation (**UNT$_{\mathbf{L}}$**) which is influenced by high capitalization.

Findings also reveal that, except for **UNT$_{\mathbf{L}}$**, return spillovers to corporation (*i*) from all other corporations are vary considerably before and during the COVID-19 crisis period, and according to the size of the corporation. Indeed, during the pre-COVID period (respectively during the COVID-19 period) 71.1% (respectively 78.9%) of the error variance in forecasting **NXT$_{\mathbf{H}}$** returns come from others, 62.9% (respectively 77%) for **DOM$_{\mathbf{H}}$**, 67.6% (respectively 80.3%) for **STH$_{\mathbf{H}}$**, 72.9%

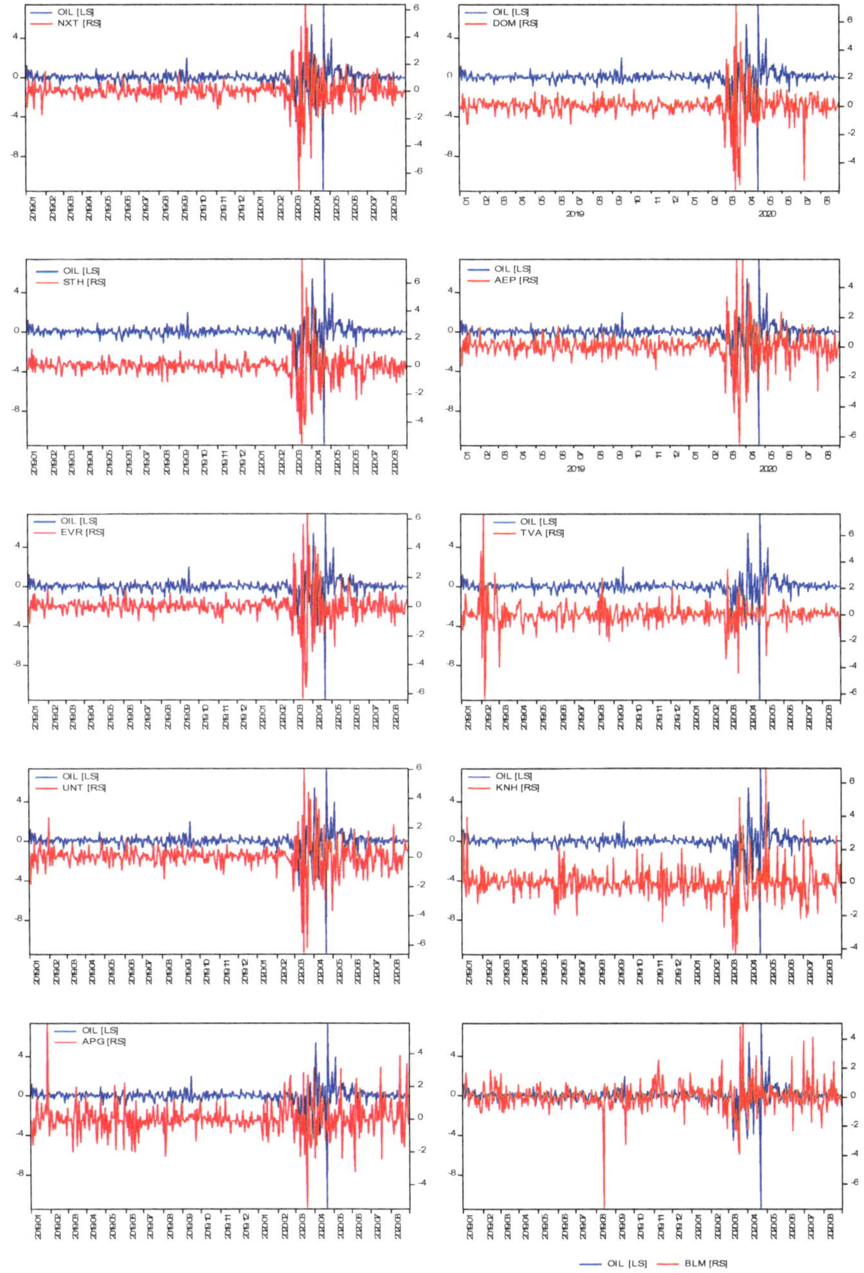

Fig. 1 Oil and stock price return. *Note* [RS] and [LS] stand respectively for "Right Scale" and "Left Scale", respectively

Table 1 Descriptive statistics, 01/01/2019—31/08/2020

	NXT_H	DOM_H	STH_H	AEP_H	EVR_H
Mean	2.76E−11	−6.90E−12	1.38E−11	−2.30E−12	6.90E−12
Median	0.000311	0.001906	0.03825	0.040134	0.003492
Maximum	6.348921	7.181144	7.704823	5.852457	6.348198
Minimum	−7.244066	−5.952712	−5.636414	−6.53423	−6.368954
Std. Dev.	1	1	1	1	1
Skewness	−0.352607	−0.423995	0.412371	−0.322178	−0.067186
Kurtosis	17.57329	19.49152	19.38126	15.27143	18.38243
Kurtosis	2.76E−11	−6.90E−12	1.38E−11	−2.30E−12	6.90E−12
	$\mathbf{TVA_L}$	$\mathbf{UNT_L}$	$\mathbf{KNH_L}$	$\mathbf{APG_L}$	$\mathbf{BLM_L}$
Mean	1.38E−11	−2.76E−11	1.38E−11	5.29E−11	5.06E−11
Median	−0.010261	0.040375	−0.032856	−0.099896	−0.014352
Maximum	7.617987	6.030213	6.856689	5.855891	5.084045
Minimum	−6.423195	−6.597792	−4.306233	−5.469507	−7.682753
Std. Dev.	1	1	1	1	1
Skewness	0.149771	−0.679871	1.077001	0.423917	−0.36136
Kurtosis	18.04499	16.75611	11.9445	8.63672	14.9383

(respectively 78.3%) for $\mathbf{AEP_H}$, 72.3% (respectively 78.9%) for $\mathbf{EVR_H}$, 65.7% (respectively 76.3%) for $\mathbf{UNT_L}$, but only 8.8% (respectively 46.6%) of $\mathbf{TVA_L}$ returns come from others, 5.8% (respectively 40.2%) for $\mathbf{KNH_L}$, 6.8% (respectively 27%) for $\mathbf{APG_L}$, 7.8% (respectively 30.7%) for $\mathbf{BLM_L}$, 9% (respectively 26.6%) for **OIL**. Likewise, for the return spillovers from each of the considered corporations (*j*) to other corporations (*i*).

Likewise, the results show the directional spillovers from each of the considered corporations (*j*) to each of the other corporations (*i*). For example, during the pre-COVID-19 period (respectively during the COVID-19 period) shocks to the **NXT** stock market returns are responsible for 13.4% (respectively 13.7%) of the error variance in forecasting 10-days-ahead $\mathbf{DOM_H}$ returns, 13.6% (respectively 15.7%) of the error variance in forecasting $\mathbf{STH_H}$ returns, 16.1% (respectively 14.7%) of the error variance in forecasting $\mathbf{AEP_H}$ returns, 16.8% (respectively 14.8%) of the error variance in forecasting $\mathbf{EVR_H}$ returns, 14.6% (respectively 15.4%) of the error variance in forecasting $\mathbf{UNT_L}$ returns, but only 1.5% (respectively 2%) of the error variance in forecasting 10-days-ahead **OIL** returns, 0.3% (respectively 6.1%) of the error variance in forecasting $\mathbf{TVA_L}$ returns, 0.1% (respectively 5.6%) of the error variance in forecasting $\mathbf{KNH_L}$ returns, 1.4% (respectively 3%) of the error variance in forecasting $\mathbf{APG_L}$ returns, and 0.6% (respectively 7.9%) of the error variance in forecasting $\mathbf{BLM_L}$ returns. From the directional spillover "contribution to others" row, we notice that, except for $\mathbf{AEP_H}$ and $\mathbf{EVR_H}$ which are largely stable between the pre-crisis and crisis periods, all other directional return spillovers to others from each of the considered electricity companies have increased significantly.

Table 2 Spillovers from return (*j*) to return (*i*)—Full sample period

To (*i*)	From (*j*)											
	OIL	NXT_H	DOM_H	STH_H	AEP_H	EVR_H	TVA_L	UNT_L	KNH_L	APG_L	BLM_L	From others
OIL	80.5	1.5	4.6	2.4	1.8	0.6	1.4	0.7	4	0.7	1.7	19.5
NXT_H	0.3	22.8	13.6	16.3	14.4	15.1	0.7	14.3	1.1	0.4	1.1	77.2
DOM_H	0.8	14	24.6	16.3	13.5	16.4	0.4	12.4	0.9	0.6	0.3	75.4
STH_H	0.4	15.6	15.2	21.3	15.4	16.4	0.4	13.2	1.1	0.3	0.8	78.7
AEP_H	0.3	15.2	13.2	16.8	23	16.3	0.6	13.2	0.7	0.3	0.3	77
EVR_H	0.1	15	15.6	16.8	15.2	22	0.3	13.9	0.3	0.4	0.3	78
TVA_L	1.3	2.6	1.7	2.4	2.8	2	81.4	3.7	1.4	0.2	0.5	18.6
UNT_L	0.2	15.6	13.1	14.8	13.3	14.9	1	25.3	0.6	0.4	0.8	74.7
KNH_L	3.7	4	3	3.7	3	1.3	1.2	1.2	73.9	2.3	2.6	26.1
APG_L	0.7	2.2	2.4	2.2	1.8	3.4	0.4	1.9	0.3	83.1	1.6	16.9
BLM_L	1.5	4.2	1.2	3	0.8	1	0.1	2.4	2.5	0.3	82.9	17.1
Contr. to others	9.3	90.1	83.5	94.6	82.1	87.5	6.6	77	12.9	5.9	9.7	**Spillover**
Contr.incl.own	89.7	112.9	108.1	115.9	105.2	109.6	87.9	102.3	86.8	89	92.6	**Index**
Net spillovers	-10.2	12.9	8.1	15.9	5.1	9.5	-12	2.3	-13.2	-11	-7.4	**50.80%**

Notes A VAR of order 1 was selected: the Bayesian Information Criterion was used to choose the lag order

Table 3 Spillovers from return (*j*) to return (*i*)—Pre-Covid-19 period

To (*i*)	From (*j*)											
	OIL	NXT_H	DOM_H	STH_H	AEP_H	EVR_H	TVA_L	UNT_L	KNH_L	APG_L	BLM_L	From others
OIL	91	1.5	0.1	1.6	0.8	1.5	0.2	0.5	1	0.1	1.7	9
NXT_H	0.6	28.9	10.4	12.1	17.2	17.5	0.2	12.3	0.1	0.4	0.2	71.1
DOM_H	0.5	13.4	37.1	10.5	15	13.2	0.1	9.6	0.4	0.1	0.1	62.9
STH_H	0.3	13.6	9.1	32.4	17.1	15.9	0.1	9.8	0.6	0.4	0.7	67.6
AEP_H	0.3	16.1	11	14.3	27.1	18.6	0.2	11.9	0	0.2	0.3	72.9
EVR_H	0.4	16.8	9.8	13.6	19.1	27.7	0.2	11.8	0	0.3	0.3	72.3
TVA_L	0.3	0.3	1.1	0	0.4	0.7	91.2	4.3	0.1	0.3	1.4	8.8
UNT_L	0.2	14.6	8.8	10.1	15.1	14.6	1.4	34.3	0.1	0.7	0.1	65.7
KNH_L	1.2	0.1	0.7	2	0.1	0.1	0.3	0.3	94.2	0.7	0.4	5.8
APG_L	0.1	1.4	0.2	0.8	0.3	2.2	0.3	0.7	0.5	93.2	0.2	6.8
BLM_L	0.4	0.6	0.7	1.7	1.2	1	1.3	0.5	0.4	0.1	92.2	7.8
Contr. to others	4.2	78.4	51.8	66.7	86.4	85.2	4.4	61.8	3.2	3.3	5.5	**Spillover**
Contr.incl.own	95.2	107.3	88.9	99.1	113.4	112.9	95.6	96.1	97.3	96.5	97.6	**Index**
Net spillovers	-4.8	7.3	-11.1	-0.9	13.5	12.9	-4.4	-3.9	-2.6	-3.5	-2.3	**41.00%**

Notes A VAR of order 1 was selected: the Bayesian Information Criterion was used to choose the lag order

Table 4 Spillovers from Return (*j*) to Return (*i*) - Covid-19 Period

To (*i*)	From (*j*)											From others
	OIL	NXT_H	DOM_H	STH_H	AEP_H	EVR_H	TVA_L	UNT_L	KNH_L	APG_L	BLM_L	
OIL	73.4	2	5	3	2.4	0.8	3.9	1	4.6	1	2.8	26.6
NXT_H	0.4	21.1	13.3	16.4	13.7	14.3	2.3	14.1	1.7	0.6	2.2	78.9
DOM_H	0.8	13.7	23	16.4	13.1	16	1.8	12.7	1.1	0.9	0.5	77
STH_H	0.5	15.7	15.3	19.7	15	15.9	1.8	13.4	1.5	0.4	0.9	80.3
AEP_H	0.5	14.7	13.1	16.7	21.7	15.4	2.3	13.1	1.3	0.5	0.7	78.3
EVR_H	0.1	14.8	15.9	16.7	14.7	21.1	1.1	14	0.4	0.6	0.6	78.9
TVA_L	2.4	6.1	5.5	7	7.5	4.6	53.4	5	5.1	0.1	3.1	46.6
UNT_L	0.3	15.4	13.4	15.1	12.9	14.6	1.9	23.7	0.8	0.4	1.5	76.3
KNH_L	3.8	5.6	3.6	4.7	4.7	2.1	5.9	2.1	59.8	3	4.7	40.2
APG_L	1	3	3.7	2.9	2.8	4.4	1.2	2.7	0.6	73	4.7	27
BLM_L	2.5	7.9	1.9	3.2	1.7	1.8	3.1	4.1	4.4	0.2	69.3	30.7
Contr. to others	12.3	98.9	90.7	102	88.6	89.9	25.2	82.1	21.6	7.7	21.7	**Spillover Index**
Contr. incl.own	85.7	120	113.7	121.7	110.3	111	78.6	105.7	81.4	80.8	91	**58.30%**
Net spillovers	- 14.3	20	13.7	21.7	10.3	11	-21.4	5.8	-18.6	-19.3	-9	

Notes A VAR of order 1 was selected: the Bayesian Information Criterion was used to choose the lag order

From the net spillover indices, which are the differences between the "to" and the "from" directional spillovers, we also notice that, for both the pre-COVID-19 and the COVID-19 periods, **OIL** is not a net volatility transmitter but rather a net volatility receiver (−4.8% during the pre-COVID-19 period and −14.3% during the COVID-19 period), suggesting that OIL volatility is impacted by the electricity companies' volatilities and this impact is even more important during the COVID-19 crisis period. This result may also indicate that there was probably a negative bubble in oil prices in 2019–2020, which caused them to fall below the level justified by economic fundamentals and which could explain the weak spillovers. Furthermore, at the company level, $\mathbf{AEP_H}$ and $\mathbf{EVR_H}$ are the main net volatility transmitters to all other firms during the pre-COVID-19 period (13.5% and 12.9%, respectively), and $\mathbf{STH_H}$ and $\mathbf{NXT_H}$ are the main net volatility transmitters to all other firms during the COVID-19 crisis (21.7% and 20%, respectively). On the opposite side, $\mathbf{DOM_H}$, $\mathbf{TVA_L}$ and $\mathbf{UNT_L}$ are the main net volatility receivers from all other firms during the pre-COVID-19 crisis (−11.1%, −4.4% and −3.9% respectively), while $\mathbf{TVA_L}$, $\mathbf{APG_L}$, $\mathbf{KNH_L}$ and **OIL** are the main receivers during the COVID-19 crisis (−21.4%, −19.3%, −18.6% and −14.3%, respectively).

Despite the interesting findings reported in Tables 2, 3 and 4, we should emphasize on the fact that these are static volatility spillovers. However, the shift of the intensities of the static spillovers between the pre-COVID-19 period and the COVID-19 crisis period shows that the relationship between **OIL** and electricity firm-level volatilities is time-varying, and suggests that the static spillover index do not provides do not accuracy captures the effects of the financial and economic developments characterizing the period examined. Thus, to corroborate this assertion, it is important to examine how volatility spillovers evolved over time by using a dynamic rolling-sample analysis. As in Diebold and Yilmaz (2012), we now estimate the total time-varying volatility spillover using rolling windows of different sizes (50, 100, 150 and 200-day) to check robustness.

Figure 2 presents the total time-varying spillover index based on rolling windows of different sizes and 10-day-ahead forecast horizon. A first broad observation shows that spillovers have a very similar time pattern regardless the size of the rolling window. It is interesting to note that despite the fact that the static total spillover is estimated to be 50.8% on average over the full sample period, when we examine this index over time we are able to see that it actually fluctuates at a relatively high level for highest capitalizations (from about 50% to almost 80%), which reflects the high level of integration among the large electricity firms, but at a relatively low level for lowest capitalizations (from about 10% to almost 55%), which reflects the relatively low level of integration among the small electricity firms. The significant increase in spillovers during the COVID-19 medical shock reflects the strength of the link

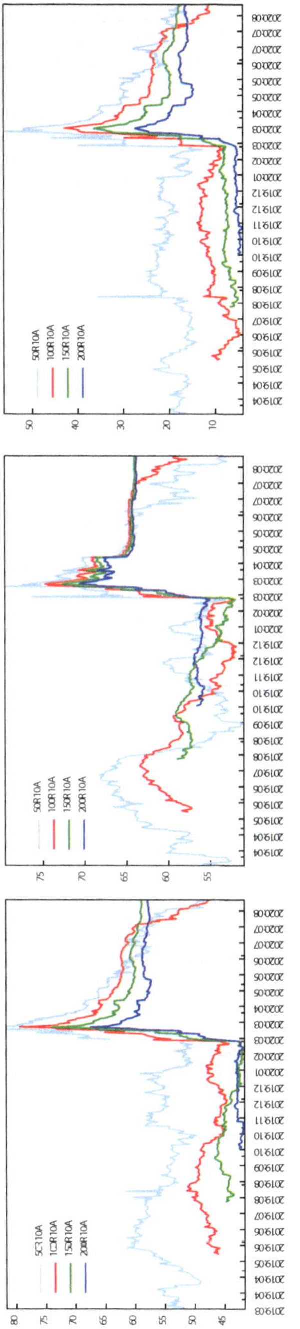

Fig. 2 Spillover plots. *Note* All capitalizations (Left), highest capitalizations (Middle) and lowest capitalizations (Right). To check robustness, the drifting spillover indices was estimated using different rolling windows (50, 100, 150 and 200) and ten-days-ahead forecast horizon

between the electricity firms during extreme events and their exposure to the same shocks, as well as the uncertainty in the U.S. stock market due to the epidemic shock. We note that the total volatility spillover began to display an upward momentum since late February 2020, before reaching its peak towards early March. Interestingly, the spillover effects dissipated immediately and quickly after reaching its peak. A plausible explanation of such behavior can be found in the economic measures that have been taken by governments and central banks following the COVID-19 pandemic to limit the human and economic impact. Such economic measures include: (**a**) the use of US$44 billion from the DRF (Disaster Relief Fund) to provide extra unemployment benefit; (**b**) further student loan payment relief; (**c**) US$4.8 trillion to help and assist small businesses and hospitals, to expand virus testing, to provide a food safety-net for the most vulnerable people, and to assist overseas countries (See the Paycheck Protection Program and Health Care Enhancement Act and the CARES Act); (**d**) the easing of monetary policy (e.g. the reduction of the Federal Funds Rate by 150 bp in March, the extension of repos, the introduction of new facilities to support credit, etc.).

4 Concluding Remarks

Our study asses the risk transmission across oil market and U.S. electricity market from 1st January 2019 to 31 August 2020 by using Diebold and Yilmaz's (2012) spillover index. We select the crude oil Brent as our benchmark and five electricity companies that have the highest market capitalization and five others that have the lowest, given that crisis's impact may depend on the company size. Our findings are reported into two levels. Firstly, our static investigation shows that the volatility spillovers are important during the full sample period but more intense during COVID-19 pandemic. From a global view, companies with high capitalization are rather influenced by other companies having high capitalization, while companies with low capitalization are influenced by other companies having low capitalization. As for the oil market, the Brent volatility is impacted by the electricity companies' volatilities and this impact is even more important during the COVID-19 crisis period. Secondly, our dynamic analysis, based on the spillover plots, reflects the same spillover patters regardless the size of the rolling window. The dynamic index fluctuates highly indicating the high level of integration among the large electricity firms, but at a relatively low level for lowest capitalizations.

For future works, it would be interesting to investigate the hedging effect in addition to spillover impacts that is crucial for investors to adjust their investments.

References

Abu-Rayash A, Dincer I (2020) Analysis of the electricity demand trends amidst the COVID-19 coronavirus pandemic. Energy Res Soc Sci 68. https://doi.org/10.1016/j.erss.2020.101682

Antonakakis N, Cunado J, Filis G, Gabauer D, Perez de Gracia F (2018) Oil volatility, oil and gas firms and portfolio diversification. Energy Econ 70:499–515. https://doi.org/10.1016/j.eneco.2018.01.023

Ben Amar A, Bélaïd F, Ben Youssef A, Chiao B, Guesmi K (2020) The unprecedented equity and commodity markets reaction to COVID-19. SSRN Working Paper. https://dx.doi.org/10.2139/ssrn.3606051

Diebold FX, Yilmaz K (2012) Better to give than to receive: predictive directional measurement of volatility spillovers. Int J Forecast 28(1):57–66. https://doi.org/10.1016/j.ijforecast.2011.02.006

Dutta A, Das D, Jana RK, Vo XV (2020) COVID-19 and oil market crash: revisiting the safe haven property of gold and bitcoin. Resour Policy. 69. https://doi.org/10.1016/j.resourpol.2020.101816

Figueroa J, Counts T, Graves F, Mudge B, Pant S (2020) Impact of COVID-19 on the US energy industry. The Brattle group, February/March Assessment. https://brattlefiles.blob.core.windows.net

Gharib C, Mefteh-Wali S, Ben Jabeur S (2020) The bubble contagion effect of COVID-19 outbreak: evidence from crude oil and gold markets. Finance Res Lett. https://doi.org/10.1016/j.frl.2020.101703

IEA (2020) Covid-19 impact on electricity. IEA, Paris. https://www.iea.org/reports/covid-19-impact-on-electricity

Koop G, Pesaran MH, Potter SM (1996) Impulse response analysis in nonlinear multivariate models. J Econometrics 74:119–147. https://doi.org/10.1016/0304-4076(95)01753-4

Mensi W, Sensoy A, Vo XV, Kang SH (2020) Impact of COVID-19 outbreak on asymmetric multifractality of gold and oil prices. Resour Policy 69. https://doi.org/10.1016/j.resourpol.2020.101829

Mzoughi H, Urom C, Uddin GS, Guesmi K (2020) The effects of COVID-19 pandemic on oil prices, CO_2 emissions and the stock market: evidence from a VAR model. http://dx.doi.org/10.2139/ssrn.3587906

Norouzi N, Fani M (2020) The impacts of the novel corona virus on the oil and electricity demand in Iran and China. J Energy Manag Technol 4(4), http://dx.doi.org/10.22109/jemt.2020.222593.1232

Norouzi N, Zarazua de Rubens G, Choubanpishehzafar S, Enevoldsen P (2020) When pandemics impact economies and climate change: exploring the impacts of COVID-19 on oil and electricity demand in China. Energy Res Soc Sci 68. https://doi.org/10.1016/j.erss.2020.101654

Pesaran HH, Shin Y (1998) Generalized impulse response analysis in linear multivariate models. Econ Lett 58:17–29. https://doi.org/10.1016/S0165-1765(97)00214-0

Sadorsky P (2012) Correlations and volatility spillovers between oil prices and the stock prices of clean energy and technology companies. Energy Econo 34(1), https://doi.org/10.1016/j.eneco.2011.03.006

Salisu AA, Ebuh GU, Usman N (2020) Revisiting oil-stock nexus during COVID-19 pandemic: some preliminary results. Int Rev Econ Finance 69:280–294. https://doi.org/10.1016/j.iref.2020.06.023

Sharif A, Aloui C, Yarovaya L (2020) COVID-19 pandemic, oil prices, stock market, geopolitical risk and policy uncertainty nexus in the US economy: fresh evidence from the wavelet-based approach. Inter Rev Finan Anal 70. https://doi.org/10.1016/j.irfa.2020.101496

Wang J, Shao W, Kim J (2020) Analysis of the impact of COVID-19 on the correlations between crude oil and agricultural futures. Chaos, Solitons Fractals 136. https://doi.org/10.1016/j.chaos.2020.109896

World Bank (2020) A shock like no other: the impact of COVID-19 on commodity markets, commodity markets outlook, April 2020

Hela Mzoughi is currently a Ph.D. and Assistant Professor at Carthage Business School, University of Tunis Carthage. She earned her Ph.D. in Management from Higher Management Science of Sousse in January 2016 and she is specialized on Quantitative methods. Her master Research degree is in Actuarial Sciences and Finance from High Commercial Studies Institute of Sousse. Her research interests are quantitative finance, risk management and actuarial science.

Amine Ben Amar is Currently Professor of Economics at the International University of Rabat [RBS College of Management], A. Ben Amar has a Ph.D. in Economics from Paris-Dauphine University (France). Amine Ben Amar's recent research interests include applied and computational economics with a special focus on environmental economics, monetary policy transmission channels, financial markets, and commodity markets.

Challenges of Renewable Energy to Sustainable Development: Post-Coronavirus' Economic Recovery Plan

Narjess Aloui, Imen Sdiri, and Rafla Hchaichi

Abstract COVID-19 pandemic has devastated several industries, and energy is no exception. This chapter reflects a wide reviewing of the effect of COVID-19 on the renewable energy transition, ranging from risks to opportunities of investing in renewable energy projects. In response to the pandemic, decision-makers are invited to focus on financial risks, trust, public acceptance, and technical skills among other challenges and risks.

Keywords COVID-19 · Renewable energies · Investments · Risks and opportunities

1 Introduction

For years, the concept of renewable energy predates current climate awareness and improvement debates. This explains, to some extent, why the concept is problematic in today's context. Climate and covid-19 crises reveal the need to increase climate ambition and shift the world's energy supplies towards renewable. Comparing to energy derived from fossil fuels, obviously clean energy is better for the planet. It helps avoiding greenhouse gas emissions, generate cleaner air and deliver energy to marginalized communities. In response to the exceptional circumstances stemming from the coronavirus pandemic, renewable energy seems to be the perfect solution for the economic recovery plan post covid-19. Indeed, the Covid-19 crises cost jobs and economic growth for most countries around the world, which pushed governments to inject fortunes into their economies to rise again.

N. Aloui (✉)
University of Tunis Carthage-Carthage Business School, GEMAS Lab, FSEG, Tunis, Tunisia
e-mail: Narjes.aloui@utctunisie.com

I. Sdiri
Carthage University, ISG Bizerte, URCC Lab, FSEG, Tunis, Tunisia

R. Hchaichi
University of Tunis Carthage-Carthage Business School, ESCTRA Lab IHEC, Carthage, Tunisia

S. Goutte et al. (eds.), *Advances in Managing Energy and Climate Risks*,
Lecture Notes in Energy 82, https://doi.org/10.1007/978-3-030-71403-1_3

This chapter shows the role of renewable energy as an alternative to generate a strong capacity for governments to heal from crises.

As the technology keeps improving, solar and wind energy are taking place of the high-cost electricity. According to the 2020 Global Trends in Renewable Energy Investment report, the new solar photovoltaic plants provide 83% lower cost electricity in 2019.

Investment in renewable energy projects is now outpacing investment in new fossil fuel-powered generation capacity: in 2018, global investment in renewable energy capacity hit $272.9 billion, far outstripping investments in new fossil fuel generation according to the 2019 Global Trends in Sustainable Energy Investment report published by the United Nations Environment Program and Bloomberg New Energy Finance.

This surge in investment is not a surprising phenomenon especially after the slump in the fossil fuel sector due to Covid-19, which made clean energy an intelligent investment.

More initiative from governments to put clean energy at the heart of Covid-19 economic recovery, instead of financing the recovery of fossil-fuel industries, can improve access to energy for most of the population, reduce emissions of local and global pollutants, and may create local socio-economic development opportunities, and ultimately are the best insurance policy against global pandemics.

Nevertheless, the major challenge for developing countries is access to financial resources by multiple parties, at varying points in the project life cycles.

Under circumstances as these, developing countries remain the most gifted with a huge and still unused renewable energy potential. Estimates of power generation potential in the continent are 350 GW for hydroelectric, 110 GW for wind, 15 GW for geothermal, and a staggering 1000 GW for solar (African Development Bank 2017). The potential for bioenergy is also high, with wood supply from surplus forest estimated at 520 GWh/year (International Renewable Energy Agency 2015). Solar is particularly promising in terms of geographical distribution: '*albeit with varying potentials, this type of energy could be harnessed virtually everywhere in Africa*'.

This chapter contributes to a better understanding of opportunities and the challenges to put renewable energy at the heart of the Covid-19 economic recovery plan.

2 The Impact of COVID-19 on the Ongoing Renewable Energy Projects

THE recent COVID-19 pandemic has affected people's lives resulted in the deaths of millions of people, international market situations, and energy industries (Anderson et al. 2020; Nicola et al. 2020). The consequences of the COVID-19 spread are expected to be even more pervasive over time. Trillions of dollars were prompted by governments and institutions to support the current situation and save people's lives. A dramatic situation pushed some businesses to shut down their stores and cost workers their jobs. The current situation has devastated several industries and the global energy system is no exception. Countries over the world have practiced self-isolation which spontaneously caused a considerable improvement of environmental pollution by reducing fuel consumption (Chen et al. 2020). Despite the flourished scenario of global renewable energy in recent decades, the coronavirus has generated a serious challenge for energy manufacturing facilities and slowed down the transition to renewables. Due to the crisis, many renewable energy projects will certainly be delayed. Taking the example of the American-based Morgan Stanley Company that decides to reduce the installation of the US solar photovoltaics (PVs) in the second, third, and fourth quarters of 2020 by 48%, 28%, and 17% respectively (P. Fox-Penner 2020).

The coronavirus has strengthened the under-construction REPs and weakened the fossil fuel demand which been resulted in a remarkable reduction in the fossil fuel price, particularly in developing countries. Due to their poor economic situation, the developing countries are more sensitive to the energy cost that could compel their governments to adopt cheaper conventional energy sources instead of renewable energy. This decision could be fearful of global climate policy but could be prevented if banks communicate lower interest rates for REPs.

Yet before the COVID situation, the transition to RE becomes more affordable for many countries given to their progressive awareness, the downturn in technologies' cost, and the substantial innovations. According to Hosseini and Wahid (2016), solar and wind power have become cheaper in recent years, and it was expected that erelong the renewables would outpace fossil fuels because most investment in renewables comes from outside the fossil fuel sectors.

According to the International Renewable Energy Agency's (IRENA)[1] report 2020, the global renewable energy capacity hit 2537 GW (GW) at the end of 2019, which illustrates a 176 GW increase compared to 2018. The statistics indicate that 72% of all electrical power expansion in 2019 was due to development in the renewables, of which the wind and solar energies grew 60 GW and 90 GW respectively and together were responsible for 90% of renewable additions.

Based on the Global Wind Energy Council's (GWEC) report 2020, 70% of the wind power new capacity in 2019 was installed in China, the U.S., U.K., India, and Spain, all of which are suffering from ongoing COVID-19 pandemic. The GWEC has postulated that disruptions to worldwide supply chains due to the COVID-19 will certainly influence the implementation of wind energy projects in 2020. Despite the ongoing crisis, 96% of the wind manufacturing sites in Europe remain open. This proves that despite the confinement of all countries, renewable energy projects

[1]IRENA: International Renewable energy Agency is an intergovernmental organization that supports countries in their transition to a sustainable energy future, and serves as the principal platform for international cooperation, a center of excellence, and financial knowledge on renewable energy.

do not depend on teams' presence. Indeed, the share of renewables in the first three months of 2020 reached 41% (*16% more than the amount generated in the first quarter of 2019*) owing to a sudden fall in demand and prices. In February 2020, Germany, Ireland, and Denmark supplied 50% of their electricity demand for wind energy (REW 2020).

3 Risks and Barriers to Renewable Energy

3.1 Renewable Energy Policies and Barriers

Since the '90s, energy policies have witnessed an explosion around the world. The change in energy regulation has been driven by several components like environmental, economic, trust, and public concerns. Many of these changes have promoted the need for REPs. Yet, the development of new renewable energy projects has been affected by many policies and barriers. Beck and Martinot (2004) have resumed these policies in six direct and indirect policies: renewable energy promotion policies, transport biofuels policies, emissions reduction policies, electric power restructuring policies, distributed generation policies, and rural electrification policies. Investors and decision-makers are invited to use manage these policies to reduce barriers that impede the development of renewable energy projects.

Table 1 resumed these barriers according to Beck and Martinot (2004) policies and barriers.

One of the most important stimuli for decision-makers is cost. It presents one of the investment barriers along with employees' skills and relationship with power producers. Most policies addressed the importance of financial, public, and technical perceived risks. Other policies have the same importance such as trust, public acceptance, and technical barriers. For decision-makers, those policies could strengthen the barriers instead of reducing them.

3.2 Trust and Public Acceptance Risks

To face the challenges of the energy transition, renewable energy is perceived as an alternative of fossil fuels and nuclear energy. Renewable energy projects (REP) are not only changing people and society life but also, they are affecting every sector of the economy. People's awareness is growing, along with their demands and expectations. It is a good reason why, so many industry sectors are investing in new and emerging energy technologies. Renewable energy is a widely used term that describes certain types of energy production and it highly participates in global climate change as a key solution.

Table 1 Summary of renewable energy policies and barriers

Policies	Description	Key barriers addressed
Renewable energy promotion policies		
Price-setting and quantity-forcing policies	Mandates prices to be paid for renewable energy, or requires a fixed amount or share of generation to be renewable	High costs, unfavorable power pricing rules, perceived risks
Cost reduction policies	Reduces investment costs through subsidies, rebates, tax relief, loans, and grants	High costs, perceived risks
Public investments and market facilitation activities	Provides public funds for direct investments or for guarantees, information, training, etc. to facilitate investments	Transaction costs, perceived risks, lack of access to credit, information, and skills
Power grid access policies	Gives renewable energy equal or favorable treatment for access to power grids and transmission systems	Independent power producer frameworks, transmission access, inter-connection requirements
Transport biofuels policies		
Biofuels mandates	Mandates specific shares of transport fuel consumption from biofuels	Lack of fuel production or delivery infrastructure
Biofuel tax policies	Provides tax relief for biofuels	High costs
Emissions reduction policies		
Renewable energy set- asides	Allocates, or sets aside, a percentage of mandated environmental emissions reductions to be met by renewable energy	Environmental externalities
Emissions cap and trade policies	Allows renewables to receive monetary credit for local pollutant emissions reductions	Environmental externalities
Greenhouse gas mitigation policies	Allows renewables to receive monetary credit for greenhouse-gas emissions reductions	Environmental externalities
Power sector restructuring policies		
Competitive wholesale power markets	Allows competition in supplying wholesale generation to the utility network and eliminates wholesale pricing restrictions	May heighten barriers of high costs, lack of fuel price risk assessment, unfavorable power pricing rules

(continued)

Table 1 (continued)

Policies	Description	Key barriers addressed
Self-generation by end- users	Allows end-users to generate their own electricity and either sell surplus power back to the grid or partly offset purchased power	May reduce barrier of inter-connection requirements, but heighten barriers of high costs, lack of fuel price risk assessment
Privatization and/or Commercialization of utilities	Changes government-owned and operated utilities into private or commercial entities	May reduce barrier of subsidies, but heighten barriers of high capital costs and perceived risks
Unbundling of generation, transmission and distribution	Eliminates monopolies so that separate entities provide generation, transmission, and distribution	May provide greater incentives to self-generate, including with renewable energy
Competitive retail power markets	Provides competition at the retail level for power sales, including "green power" sales	May reduce barriers of high costs, lack of information, transaction costs
Distributed generation policies		
Net metering	Values renewable energy production at the point of end-use and allow utility networks to provide "energy storage" for small users	Unfavorable power pricing rules
Real-time pricing	Values renewable energy production at the actual cost of avoided fossil fuel generation at any given time of the day	Unfavorable power pricing rules
Capacity credit	Provides credit for the value of standing renewable energy capacity, not just energy Production	Unfavorable power pricing rules
Interconnection regulations	Creates consistent and transparent rules, norms, and standards for interconnection	Interconnection requirements, transaction costs
Rural electrification policies		
Rural electrification policy and energy service concessions	Makes renewable energy part of rural electrification policy and planning and creates regulated businesses to serve rural customers	Subsidies for competing fuels, lack of skills and information, high costs, lack of access to credit

(continued)

Table 1 (continued)

Policies	Description	Key barriers addressed
Rural business development and microcredit	Supports private entrepreneurs to provide renewable energy products and services to end-users and offer consumer credit for purchases	Lack of skills, lack of access to credit
Comparative line extension analyses	Analyzes the relative costs of renewable energy with conventional fuels and power delivery	Subsidies for competing fuels, lack of information

Source Beck and Martinot (2004)

REPs are exposed to market risks starting by the community acceptance to financial investments. Understanding the vital role of public acceptance for RES and its implications for realizing the projects are important.

According to the RE act, renewable energy provides more than half of electricity consumption around the world. Giving the high potential need for energy, infrastructure technologies are required (Tomescu et al. 2017). The majority of citizens are in favor of using renewable energies instead of fossil fuels and nuclear energy. Nevertheless, same community objects and protests the required large-scale infrastructure elements (Cain and Nelson 2013; Reusswig et al. 2016).

Studies have proved a positive relationship between risk perceptions and perceived benefits along with trust to affect the acceptance of large-scale infrastructure technologies (Nelson et al. 2018). This relationship presents valuable information for investors and technology designers to pre-identify the concerns of citizens to infrastructure planning, communication and information needs (Huijts et al. 2012; Ashworth et al. 2010). Public perceptions of project risks refer generally to their evaluation of the possible consequences of these projects (Sjöberg et al. 2020). In the absence of knowledge people tend to less trust technologies and perceived more risks, although it may be surprising that with a higher trust in involved actors, people tend to higher perceive benefit and diminish perceived risks to accept new technology (Siegrist and Cvetkovich 2000; Liu et al. 2019). Several researches have proved the mediation role of trust on perceptions and acceptance of large-scale energy technologies (e.g., for the energy transition in general (Gölz and Wedderhoff 2018), for wind power (Rand and Hoen 2017), for nuclear power plants (Oltra et al. 2019), or transmission lines (Nelson et al. 2018). The most knowing risks related to energy infrastructure are noise emissions (wind power (Songsore and Buzzelli 2014), (Wadley et al. 2019), environmental consequences of the wind power on animals, especially birds (Reusswig et al. 2016; Baxter et al. 2013). Comparing to different large-sale technologies such as nuclear power and fossil fuels, REPs were evaluated as the less risky technology (Burger 2012; Visschers and Siegrist 2014).

3.3 Financial Risks

For most decision makers, minimizing the financial risks and obtain maximum of gain is one of the primary concerns followed by the underlying investment framework (Amin et al. 2014). Several risks challenge the industry as it grows including tariffs, opposition from the fossil fuel industry, and the vulnerability of supply chains that are all concerns for the renewable energy industry. Financial inducements play a crucial role in the development of Green or renewable technology. They remain the key obstacle to implement the renewable energy industry due to the lack of long-term funding with low-cost. It becomes critical in the least developed countries whose macroeconomic conditions are unfavorable. In Africa, the governments don't allocate sufficient budget to the renewable energy industry.

However, the implementation of the renewable projects requires materials with high cost that burden on foreign exchange reserves in African countries and need sustainable subsidies (Karekezi and Kithyoma 2002). Banks are reluctant to finance renewable energy projects because of the lack of knowledge of the prerequisite. Consequently, rigorous conditions including feasibility study and land titles as collateral are required to have funds. Investors are dissuaded to create projects that only benefit the wealthy population because of the tariffs (Turyareeba 1993).

High investment costs challenge the renewable energy industry. The production cost of renewable energy is relatively high; therefore, market prices remain relatively high and unaffordable to many customers, especially in the developing countries. As many investors opt for cheaper projects, the industry of renewable energy undergoes unfair competition from fossil fuel technologies whose implementation and operational costs are usually subsidized (Fashina et al. 2019).

The lack of successful and replicable renewable energy models can hinder the adoption of these technologies. Indeed, a country's economy can hinder the implementation of renewable energy technologies, particularly, in the developing countries in Sub-Saharan Africa, that we noted a great distortion in the renewable energy market. It turns out that it is crucial that governments should support renewable energy investment.

3.4 Technical Risk

The successful implementation of renewable energy technology required skilled manpower. Despite the Africans government's effort, technical knowledge remains insufficient; there is a shortage of analysts, managers, and engineers able to manage and to build sustainable projects of renewable energy (Baguant and Manrakhan 1994). For instance, the Kenyan government lacks experts in wind pumps (Harries 2002). In Zambia's government, only one engineer was responsible to manage renewable energy project (Kayo 2002). The wind project financed by the United Kingdom in Seychelles has failed due to the lack of skilled experts (Razanajatovo et al. 1994).

The failed of the renewable energy industry is giving to a managerial problem and a lack of trained personnel to operate, and to implement renewable energy activities.

Technical barriers to renewable energy development include inadequate infrastructure and a lack of investment in technology researches in renewable energy especially in regions with low education levels (Fashina et al. 2019). The lack of adequate logistics and distribution networks challenge the diffusion of renewable energy technology in developing countries, include a high transmission loss when energy is transported from the production points to consumption points. Consequently, investors are not motivated to invest in renewable energy because of the fear of losing.

Additionally, maintenance's service of equipment of renewable energy technologies turns out inadequate that hinder their adoption. Indeed, the lack of spare parts and adequate skills to repair and to maintain the equipment can lead to shortage the supply chain of renewable energy. Most investors are dissuaded to develop renewable energy technologies in developing countries.

4 The Opportunities of the Transition to Renewable Energies: Covid-19 Context

The consequences from the coronavirus are extensive, with an adverse influence on the environment. They have highlighted the need for the transition towards renewable energies. The Covid-19 pandemic has manifested the immense crisis that humanity has been experiencing for a long time. While a lot has been happened to enable renewable energy, challenges regard pollution; unrecyclable waste and forest deterioration are pervasive and shared due to our way of treating nature. However, an intelligent reaction can convert these threats to great opportunities. Indeed, the pandemic has forced many countries to apply containment measures and to limit various activities to restrictions.

One of the important effects of these measures has been a 6% drop in global energy demand and an 8% decrease in greenhouse gas emissions. However, the confinement has proved the importance of electricity and so the need to produce it from alternative energies. Wind stations and photovoltaic do not require on-site management teams, which considerably limits the direct contact between employees. Adopting renewables can be a substantial solution during the post-COVID-19. According to the latest report of IRENA, the world is expected to witness an increase in the share of renewable energies up to 80% by 2050.

As COVID-19 hits the fossil fuel industry, a new report shows that renewables are more profitable than ever, they provide an opportunity to prioritize clean energy in the economic industry (UNEP, BNEF, and FS- UNEP 2020). The deployment of sustainable energy technologies has been driven by two main reasons. The first one is linked to the growing concern to achieve sustainable development. The second reason concerns the emergence of the concepts of "green recovery" and "green economy" that was powered during the economic crisis of 2008 which is the most serious crisis since that of 1929 caused by the *subprime market* in the United States. The uncertainties of the Covid-19 crises are still major and evolving today and adopting renewables policies could be helpful.

4.1 The Contribution of Renewable Energies to Reducing GHG Emissions

Dincer (2000) claimed that there is a deep link between the use of renewable energies and sustainable development. In fact, renewable energies are one of the most effective solutions to today's environmental problems. The use of renewable energies is necessary to reduce CO_2 emissions (Mathews 2014). Dincer (2000) presented a detailed analysis of the environmental impacts of the massive use of fossil fuels. The most dangerous impacts are acid, the deterioration of the Ozone layer, and the greenhouse' effect. He concluded that the best possible solution for these problems is the use of renewable energies. The relationship between renewable energies and sustainable development was first analyzed on the basis of a case study of the city of Saarbrücken in Germany in 1980; its energy program won "*the local government honor*" during the Rio conference in 1992.

Dincer and Rosen (1999) argued the strong link between energies, the environment, and sustainable development. They considered that a society that aims to achieve sustainable development must use renewable energies because of their positive impacts on the environment. Kalogirou (2004) studied the environmental problems caused by the use of fossil fuels. Based on his study, using solar energy to heat buildings and to heat water can prevent large amounts of GHG emissions. Indeed, he claimed that GHG reduction is the main benefit of using solar energy and solar energy systems should be used as much as possible to achieve sustainable development.

While most of the studies have concentrated on the generality of the concept, few of them have focused on specific regions and/or specific renewable energy sector to determine their impact on climate change mitigation. Researches like (Yüksel 2008; Kaygusuz 2009) focused on the developing countries and emerging countries, especially those with significant renewable energy potential.

Bilen et al. (2008) addressed the need to use renewable energies in Turkey to reduce GHG emissions and participate in limiting the magnitude of climate change, especially that Turkey enjoys a strategic geographical location. Yu and Qu (2013) deal with the case of China, which is the largest emitter of CO_2 in the world. Their analysis suggests that wind power and solar power can be used as effective tools to reduce CO_2 emissions and mitigate the disastrous effects of climate change.

The cost of electricity continues to fall for wind and solar, due to technological improvements and the fierce competition in auctions. Electricity costs from new solar PV farms in the second half of 2019 were 83% lower than ten years earlier (UNEP, BNEF and FS-UNEP 2020). "*More voices are being raised to call on governments to use their COVID-19 stimulus packages to create sustainable economies*" (Andersen

2020).[2] This report shows that renewable energy is one of the smartest and most profitable investments states can make under these plans.

Indeed, GHG emissions from fossil fuels are much higher than those emitted by renewable energy sources. Offshore wind technology emits the lowest level of GHG emissions (Amponsah et al. 2014). Sapkota et al. (2014) discussed the positive impacts of the use of certain renewable energies (such as biogas, micro-hydropower and solar power) in rural communities in Nepal. This study used the LEAP (Long-range Energy Alternatives Planning) model. Shafiei and Salim (2014) tried to explore the main causes of CO_2 emissions. They used a STIRPAT model based on data from OECD countries (from 1980 to 2011). Empirical results showed that the consumption of renewable energy decreases CO_2 emissions while the consumption of conventional energy increases CO_2 emissions. Yadoo and Cruickshank (2012) used sustainability indicators to study the role of renewable energy mini grids (in Nepal, Peru and Kenya) in climate change mitigation and poverty reduction.

Granovskii et al. (2007) claimed that the use of wind and solar energies, instead of natural gas, to produce electricity and hydrogen leads to a reduction in pollutant emissions. With the current costs of electricity from wind and solar, it is shown that when electricity from renewable sources replaces electricity from natural gas, the cost of reducing pollutant emissions is more than ten times lower than the cost if hydrogen from renewable sources replaces hydrogen produced from natural gas.

Creutzig et al. (2014) studied renewable energies in Europe. They believed that the transition to an energy system based on renewable energies can alleviate, at the same time, climate change and the debt crisis of the euro area. In order to promote the transition to renewable energies, they suggested, in addition to the political frameworks specific to each country, a great deal of coordination between the policies of the Member States. Therefore, the use of renewable energies is not only a path towards climate change mitigation, but it is also a means to achieve socio-economic benefits which will be detailed in the following.

4.2 The Contribution of Renewable Energies to the Social and Economic Dimensions of Sustainable Development

COVID-19 has forced businesses across industries to adapt to operational disruptions, shifts in demand, and new ways of doing business. Also, governments have introduced economic stimulus packages to help mitigate those effects. If renewable projects will be implemented with long-term strategies in mind, they could also accelerate the transition to clean energy, helping countries to step up their efforts towards sustainable and inclusive energy systems.

According to Kammen et al. (2004), the large-scale use of renewable energy systems offers several economic benefits through innovation and the creation of new jobs. Goldemberg (2006) asserts that renewable energies are a key factor in ensuring

[2] Inger Andersen: Executive Director of the United Nations Environment Program.

sustainability. Indeed, if the global energy system continues to be dominated by fossil fuels, then regional and global environmental problems and dependence on fossil fuels will persist.

Goldemberg (2006) proposes, as a solution to these problems, the increase of the share of renewable energies in the world energy system by using "top-down" policies (for example, the Kyoto Protocol) and policies of "bottom-up" type such as the "Renewable Portfolio Standard".

Sáenz et al. (2008) analyzed the impact of renewable electricity support programs on the price of electricity. They empirically analyzed the case of wind energy production in Spain. The results showed that there is a negative correlation between the promotion of wind power and the price of electricity in general.

Mathiesen et al. (2011) presented the analysis and results of the design of an energy system based on 100% renewable energy in Denmark in 2050. Results of the energy system analysis model named "Energy PLAN" showed that an energy system based on 100% renewable energy is technically possible in the future and may even have positive technological and socio-economic results. In order to determine the impact of the deployment of renewable energies on socio-economic sustainability, we need to focus on the impact of renewable energies on socio-economic indicators such as investments, general price level, wages, energy prices, and gross domestic product (GDP). However, most of the existing studies have simply focused on a single indicator which is GDP.

Chien and Hu (2007) analyzed the effects of the use of renewable energies on the technical efficiency of 45 economies between 2001 and 2002, using the "Data Envelopment Analysis" model. In this model, labor, capital stock, and energy consumption are the endogenous variables and real GDP is the only exogenous variable. The results of this study proved that increasing the use of renewable energies improve the technical efficiency of the economy while increasing the input of conventional energy decreases technical efficiency.

Chien and Hu (2008) used structural equation modeling to analyze the effect of renewables on GDP. The results showed a positive relationship between renewables and GDP (through increasing capital formation). The relationship between renewable energy consumption and GDP has been widely analyzed by different empirical studies that analyze different countries and regions. Most empirical studies have found that there is a long-term causal link between the consumption of renewable energy and GDP (Sadorsky 2009; Apergis et al. 2010; Tugcu et al. 2012; Al-Mulla et al. 2013).

Other studies have focused on the relationship between renewable energy production and GDP. For example, Abanda et al. (2012) analyzed the correlation between the production of renewable energies and the economic growth in many blocks of the African continent. They found a positive correlation between renewable energy production and GDP, except in the Southern African bloc where this correlation is negative.

4.3 The Impact of Renewable Energies on Job Creation

Jones (2009, p. 9) indicates that: "*Solar panels do not install themselves. Wind turbines don't manufacture themselves. Buildings do not weatherize and retrofit themselves. Urban trees, green roofs, and community gardens do not plant themselves. All these activities require human labor. Recognizing this simple fact helps to undermine the myth that ecological restoration must always be at odds with the economic performance*".

Adopting renewables can bring substantial solutions during the post-COVID-19. Industries can be revived by using renewable energy technologies and creating several new jobs for unemployed people. The International Renewable Energy Agency (IRENA) estimates that transforming energy systems based on renewables could boost global GDP by $98 trillion by 2050 and create 63 million new jobs globally in renewables and energy efficiency.

A study by Pollin et al. (2009) showed that solar energy generates more jobs than fossil energy. In fact, solar power creates 5.4 direct jobs per million dollars of production, while coal creates only 1.9 direct jobs and oil and gas creates only 0.8 direct jobs. Wei et al. (2010) also focused on the solar energy sector. Compared to other renewable resources, the solar PV energy sector is the most intensive labor.

Many studies have looked at the potential of creating "green" jobs in the European Union (EU). This interest is mainly due to the ambitious objectives of the EU that 20% of the produced energy by 2020 will be from renewable sources. Blanco and Rodrigues (2009) tried to estimate the number of direct jobs created in the wind energy sector in all EU countries. In Europe, Germany and Spain are the countries which have received the most interest from researchers due to their ambitious strategies and significant achievements in the field of renewable energies.

The high level of uncertainty surrounding the estimates of "green jobs" in the studies is due to various factors such as the ambiguity of the concept of "green jobs" and also the use of different models and ratios to estimate job creations (Gülen 2011; Lambert and Silva 2012). Studies that analyzed the impact of renewable energies on the labor market generally used methods that can be classified into two types: analytical methods and input-output methods. Lambert and Silva (2012) analyzed the advantages and disadvantages of these two methods. They conclude that analytical methods are more appropriate for area studies while input-output methods are more convenient for national and international studies.

There are several ways to measure jobs created in the renewable energy sector such as measuring jobs per installed MW for each year, jobs per cumulative installed MW, etc. Although measuring the number of created jobs is possible using various ratios, determining the quality of these created jobs is a delicate matter. Sastresa et al. (2010) tried to determine the quality of jobs created in the renewable energy sector using a Quality Factor for each renewable energy technology, in Aragon (Spain). The results of this study showed that wind power can generate better jobs than solar thermal and solar PV.

According to UNEP et al. (2008, p. 38), "*Green jobs span a wide array of skills, educational backgrounds, and occupational profiles*". Rifkin (2011) has also paid great attention to the quality and variety of created jobs in the renewable energy sector. In his book "*The Third Industrial Revolution: How Lateral Power is Transforming Energy, the Economy, and the World*", he connected the two technologies of the 21st century which are the internet and renewable energies. This link will change the way energy is distributed and create new types of jobs. According to Rifkin (2011), the workforce of the "3rd industrial revolution" will have to be qualified in new technical fields that of the management of the digital electricity grid.

In addition to their numerous and irreproachable advantages for achieving sustainable development, renewable energies have been seen in recent years as an essential component for "a green recovery" following the economic crisis.

5 Conclusion

All the cited initiatives such as "the new global green deal", "green growth" and "green economy" have made the renewable energy sector an essential and indispensable element. For these reasons, there has been a surge in investments in the renewable energy sector since the economic crisis. Still, falling renewable energy costs offer an opportunity to boost climate action in post-COVID-19 economic recovery plans. The continued growth of investment in the renewable energy sector is the most visible aspect of the transition to a green economy (UNEP, FSFM, and BNEF 2012). Indeed, according to PNUE (2009), fiscal incentives applied after the economic crisis should give priority to green sectors, especially renewable energies. Thanks to the incentives applied in several countries, notably in China and the United States, the renewable energy sector has been positively influenced by the economic crisis. Indeed, these are the rare sectors that have withstood the period of recession, even registering a record in 2011, with a total investment of 279 billion dollars mainly due to "green stimulus" programs.

The year 2012 was marked by the decline in the level of investments in RE. Indeed, the number of investments increased from 279 billion dollars in 2011 to 256 billion dollars. This decrease was caused by the decline in the level of investment in developed countries, which fell from 190 billion dollars in 2011 to 149 billion dollars in 2012. Indeed, most subsidy and aid programs renewable energy sector that was announced by governments, following the economic crisis, expired at the end of 2011. But it should be noted that the decline recorded in 2012 and 2013 did not last and that the renewable energy sector again recorded growth from 2014 (UNEP, FSFM, and BNEF 2015). Global investment in the renewable energy sector, excluding large hydropower projects, was around $ 270 billion in 2014, registering a 17% growth from the level of investment in 2013. This is the first increase recorded since the 2011 record ($ 279 billion). The good results recorded in 2014 are mainly due to the unprecedented increase in solar installations in China and Japan as well as offshore wind projects in Europe (UNEP, FSFM, and BNEF 2015).

In 2014, renewable energies represented 58.5% of the electricity capacity added worldwide. Wind power, solar PV power, and hydroelectricity accounted for the highest share of installed capacity (Adib et al. 2015). Another key feature of 2014 is the continued spread of renewable energy to new markets. Indeed, investment in developing countries reached 131.3 billion dollars, registering an increase of 36% compared to 2013. Investment in developed countries is around $ 138.9 billion. In advanced economies, "access" is defined by affordability. Utility bills represent a growing share of household spending, a challenge that could be exacerbated by the economic uncertainties created by COVID-19.

The decrease in the costs of solar and wind energy technologies made it possible to achieve strong momentum for these two technologies in 2014. In fact, investment in solar energy reached 149.6 billion dollars with an increase of 25% compared to 2013, while investment in the wind energy sector increased by 11% compared to 2013, registering a record of $ 99.5 billion (UNEP, FSFM, and BNEF 2015). 2014 was the year of great achievements for renewable energies. In fact, the level of investment rebounded sharply after two years of decline, with installed capacity exceeding that of fossil origin. In addition, investment in developing countries led by China has come very close to investment in developed economies. According to the Adib et al. (2015), the share of renewable energies in world electricity production reached 22.8% at the end of 2014. The share of hydropower is 16.6% while the share of other renewable energies is 6.2% (with 3.1% the share of wind energy).

Although worldwide the share of renewable energies in electricity production is quite low (6.2%), some countries have reached very satisfactory levels. We can cite, for example, Denmark with a share of wind power of 39.1% and Portugal with a share of 27%. Regarding solar PV energy, it reached 7.9% in Italy, 7.6% in Greece, and 7% in Germany, in 2014. China, the United States, Brazil, Germany, and Canada are the top five countries in terms of total installed electricity capacity from renewable sources, in 2014. At the start of 2015, 164 countries have renewable energy targets to achieve and 145 countries have established mechanisms and renewable energy support strategies (Adib et al. 2015).

However, this hard-won progress highlights the limits of dependence on incremental gains alone on existing policies and technologies to complete the transition to clean energy. It is in the emerging economies that we observe the most significant general improvements, the average ETI score of countries in the top 10 remaining constants since 2015. This is a sign of an urgent need for revolutionary solutions, a need threatened by COVID-19.

While the gaps between needs, commitments, and what is likely to be accomplished remain large, aggravated disruption from COVID-19 has destabilized the global energy system with potential short-term setbacks. Ultimately, more efforts are needed to ensure that recent momentum is not only preserved but accelerated, in order to achieve the ambitious goals required. If governments take advantage of the continued decline in renewable energy prices to place clean energy at the heart of post-COVID-19 economic recovery, they can take a big step towards a healthy natural world, which is the best insurance against global pandemics.

> The coronavirus pandemic provides an opportunity to consider unorthodox intervention in energy markets and global collaboration to support a recovery that will accelerate the energy transition once this crisis is abated. This giant reset is an opportunity to implement aggressive, forward-thinking, long-term strategies that will lead to a diverse, secure, and reliable energy system that ultimately supports the future growth of the global economy in a sustainable and equitable manner (Bocca 2020).

For investors, renewable energies represent a relatively "secure" sector which should continue, after the Covid-19, to attract funding. The climate crisis and the COVID-19 crisis, despite their different natures, are both disruptions that demand the attention of policymakers and entrepreneurs. Both demonstrate the need to increase our climate ambition and shift the global energy supply towards renewable energies.

References

Abanda H, Ng'ombe A, Keivani R, Tah J (2012) The link between renewable energy production and gross domestic product in Africa: a comparative study between 1980 and 2008. Renew Sustain Energy Rev 16(4):2147–2153. 10.1016/j.rser.2012.01.005

Adib R, Murdock HE, Appavou F, Brown A, Epp B, Leidreiter A et al (2015) Renewables 2015 global status report. REN21 Secretariat, Paris, France, 162

African Development Bank (2017) Organization for Economic Co-operation and Development, and United Nations Development Program

Al-mulali U, Fereidouni HG, Lee JY, Sab CN (2013) Examining the Bi-Directional long run relationship between renewable energy consumption and GDP growth. Renew Sustain Energy Rev 22:209–222. https://doi.org/10.1016/j.rser.2013.02.005

Amin MAM, Sanusi NA, Kusairi S, Abdallah, ZM (2014) Inverse relationship of financial risk and performance in commercial banks in Tanzania. Investment Manage Financ Innovations 11(4):279–291

Amponsah NY, Troldborg M, Kington B et al (2014) Greenhouse gas emissions from renewable energy sources: a review of lifecycle considerations. Renew Sustain Energy Rev 39:461–475. https://doi.org/10.1016/j.rser.2014.07.087

Anderson RM, Heesterbeek H, Klinkenberg D, Hollingsworth TD (2020) How will country-based mitigation measures influence the course of the COVID-19 epidemic? Lancet 395(10228):931–934

Apergis N, Payne JE, Menyah K, Wolde-rufael Y (2010) On the causal dynamics between emissions, nuclear energy, renewable energy and economic growth. Ecol Eco 69(11):2255–2260. https://doi.org/10.1016/j.ecolecon.2010.06.014

Ashworth P, Boughen N, Mayhew M, Millar F (2010) From research to action: now we have to move on CCS communication. Int J Greenh Gas Control 4(2010):426–433. https://doi.org/10.1016/j.ijggc.2009.10.012

Baguant J, Manrakhan J (1994) Issues in energy for the African region: Higher education training with particular reference to Mauritius. The University of Mauritius

Baxter J, Morzaria R, Hirsch R (2013) A case-control study of support/opposition to wind turbines: perceptions of health risk, economic benefits, and community conflict. Energy policy 61(2013):931–943. https://doi.org/10.1016/j.enpol.2013.06.050

Beck F, Martinot E (2004) Renewable energy policies and barriers. Encycl Energy, 365–383. https://doi.org/10.1016/b0-12-176480-x/00488-5

Bilen K, Ozyurt O, Bakirci K et al (2008) Energy production, consumption and environmental pollution for sustainable development: a case study in Turkey. Renew Sustain Energy Rev 12(6):1529–1561. https://doi.org/10.1016/j.rser.2007.03.003

Blanco MI, Rodrigues G (2009) Direct employment in the wind energy sector: An EU study. Energy Policy 37(8):2847–2857. https://doi.org/10.1016/j.enpol.2009.02.049
Bocca R (2020) Head of shaping the future of energy and materials, member of the executive committee. World Econ Forum, published on 13/05/2020. Available via:https://www.bioenergie-promotion.fr/wpcontent/uploads/2020/05/wef_fostering_effective_energy_transition_2020_editionbd.pdf
Burger J (2012) Rating of worry about energy sources with respect to public health, environmental health, and workers. J Risk Res 15(2012):1159–1169. https://doi.org/10.1080/13669877.2012.705316
Cain NL, Nelson HT (2013) What drives opposition to high-voltage transmission lines? Land use policy 33(2013):204–213. 10.1016/j.landusepol.2013.01.003
Chen K, Wang M, Huang C et al (2020) Air pollution reduction and mortality benefit during the COVID-19 outbreak in China. Lancet Planet Health 4(6):210–212
Chien T, Hu JL (2007) Renewable energy and macroeconomic efficiency of OECD and non OECD economies. Energy Policy 35(7):3606–3615. https://doi.org/10.1016/j.enpol.2006.12.033
Chien T, Hu JL (2008) Renewable energy: an efficient mechanism to improve GDP. Energy Policy 36(8):3045–3052. https://doi.org/10.1016/j.enpol.2008.04.012
Creutzig F, Goldschmid T, Lehmann P et al (2014) Catching two european birds with one renewable stone: mitigating climate change and eurozone crisis by an energy transition. Renew Sustain Energy Rev 38:1015–1028. https://doi.org/10.1016/j.rser.2014.07.028
Dincer I (2000) Renewable energy and sustainable development: a crucial review. Renew Sustain Energy Rev 4(2):157–175. https://doi.org/10.1016/S1364-0321(99)00011-8
Dincer I, Rosen MA (1999) Energy, environment and sustainable development. Appl Energy 64(1–4):427–440. 10.1016/S0306-2619(99)00111-7
Fashina A, Mundu M, Akiyode O et al (2019) The drivers and barriers of renewable energy applications and development in Uganda: a review. Clean Technol 1(1):9–39
Fox-penner P (2020) Will the COVID-19 pandemic slow the global shift to renewable energy. The Brink Boston University. Available via https://www.bu.edu/articles/2020/willthe-covid-19-pandemic-slow-the-global-shift-to-renewable-energy/, n.d. Accessed 11 April 2020
Global Wind Energy Council (2020) https://gwec.net/, n.d. Accessed 10 April 2020
Goldemberg J (2006) The promise of clean energy. Energy Policy 34(15):2185–2190. https://doi.org/10.1016/j.enpol.2005.03.009
Gölz S, Wedderhoff O (2018) Explaining regional acceptance of the German energy transition by including trust in stakeholders and perception of fairness as socio-institutional factors. Energy Res Soc Sci 43(2018):96–108. https://doi.org/10.1016/j.erss.2018.05.026
Granovskii M, Dincer I, Rosen MA (2007) Air pollution reduction via use of green energy sources for electricity and hydrogen production. Atmos Environ 41(8):1777–1783. https://doi.org/10.1016/j.atmosenv.2006.10.023
Gülen G (2011) Defining, measuring and predicting green jobs. center for energy economics, bureau of economic geology. The University of Texas at Austin. Available via: http://s3.documentcloud.org/documents/262778/ccc-green-jobs.pdf
Harries M (2002) Disseminating wind pumps in rural kenya—meeting rural water needsusing locally manufactured wind pumps. Energy Policy 30(11–12):1087–1094
Hosseini SE, Wahid MA (2016) Hydrogen production from renewable and sustainable energy resources: promising green energy carrier for clean development. Renew Sustain Energy Rev 57(2016). https://doi.org/10.1016/j.rser.2015.12.112
Huijts NMA, Molin EJE, Steg L (2012) Psychological factors influencing sustainable energy technology acceptance: a review-based comprehensive framework. Renew Sustain Energy Rev 16(2012):525–531. https://doi.org/10.1016/j.rser.2011.08
IRENA: International Renewable energy Agency is an intergovernmental organisation that supports countries in their transition to a sustainable energy future, and serves as the principal platform for international cooperation, a center of excellence, and financial knowledge on renewable energy. https://www.irena.org/, n.d. Accessed 10 April 2020

IRENA RES (2015) International renewable energy agency. Renewable Energy Target Setting, Abu Dhabi, UAE

Jones V (2009) Green collar jobs. Our planet. The Magazine of the United Nations Environment Programme. pp 8–9, Feb. Available via: http://www.unep.org/PDF/OurPlanet/2009/Feb/EN/OP-2009-02-en-FULLVERSION.pdf

Kalogirou SA (2004) Environmental benefits of domestic solar energy systems. Energy Conver Manag 45(18–19):3075–3092. https://doi.org/10.1016/j.enconman.2003.12.019

Kammen DM, Kapadia K, Fripp M (2004) Putting renewables to work: how many jobs can the clean energy industry generate? RAEL report, University of California, Berkeley, April. Available via: http://rael.berkeley.edu/old_drupal/sites/default/files/very-old-site/renewables.jobs.2006.pdf

Karekezi S, Kithyoma W (2002) Renewable energy strategies for rural Africa: is apv-led renewable energy strategy the right approach for providing modern energy to the rural poor of sub-Saharan Africa? Energy policy 30(11–12):1071–1086

Kaygusuz K (2009) Energy and environmental issues relating to greenhouse gas emissions for sustainable development in Turkey. Renew Sustain Energy Rev 13(1):253–270. https://doi.org/10.1016/j.rser.2007.07.009

Kayo D (2002) Power sector reforms in zimbabwe: will reforms increase electrification andstrengthen local participation? Energy policy 30(11–12):959–965

Lambert RJ, Patrícia PS (2012) The challenges of determining the employment effects of renewable energy. Renew Sustain Energy Rev 16(7):4667–4674. https://doi.org/10.1016/j.rser.2012.03.072

Lambert RJ, Silva PP (2012) The challenges of determining the employment effects of renewable energy. Renew Sustain Energy Rev 16(7):4667–4674. https://doi.org/10.1016/j.rser.2012.03.072

Liu L, Bouman T, Perlaviciute G, Steg L (2019) Effects of trust and public participation on acceptability of renewable energy projects in the Netherlands and China. Energy Res Soc Sci 53(2019):137–144. https://doi.org/10.1016/j.erss.2019.03.006

Mathews AP (2014) Renewable energy technologies: panacea for world energy security and climate change? Procedia Comput Sci 32:731–737. https://doi.org/10.1016/j.procs.2014.05.483

Mathiesen BV, Lund H, Karlsson K (2011) 100% renewable energy systems, climate mitigation and economic growth. Appl Energy 88(2):488–501. https://doi.org/10.1016/j.apenergy.2010.03.001

Nelson HT, Swanson B, Cain NL (2018) Close and connected: the effects of proximity and socialites on citizen opposition to electricity transmission lines. Environ Behav 50(2018):567–596. https://doi.org/10.1177/0013916517708598

Nicola M, Alsafi Z, Sohrabi C et al (2020) The socio-economic implications of the coronavirus and COVID-19 pandemic: a review. Int J Surgery. https://doi.org/10.1016/j.ijsu.2020.04.018

Oltra C, Sala R, Germán S, López-asensio S (2019) Trust perceptions among residents surrounding nuclear power plants: a descriptive and explanatory study. Prog Nucl Energy 113(2019):1–6. https://doi.org/10.1016/j.pnucene.2018.12.012

Pollin R, Heintz J, Garrett-peltier H (2009) The economic benefits of investing in clean energy: How the economic stimulus program and new legislation can boost U.S. economic growth and employment. Department of Economics and Political Economy Research Institute (University of Massachusetts) and Center for American Progress, June. Available via: http://www.peri.umass.edu/fileadmin/pdf/other_publication_types/green_economics/economic_benefits/economic_benefits.PDF

Programme des Nations Unies pour l'Environnement (PNUE) (2009) New Global compact: Guidance note. Mars, Genève, p 38. Available via: http://www.adequations.org/IMG/pdf/NouveauPacteVert.pdf

Rand J, Hoen B (2017) Thirty years of North American wind energy acceptance research: what have we learned? Energy Res Soc Sci 29(2017):135–148. https://doi.org/10.1016/j.erss.2017.05.019

Razanajatovo M, Juliette Y, Jean-louis A (1994) Renewable energy technologies dissemination in Seychelles. AFREPREN/FWD, Nairobi, Kenya

Renewable energy news & research| Renewables Now. https://renewablesnow.com/, n.d. Accessed April 10, 2020

Renewables achieve clean energy record as COVID-19 hits demand—Renewable Energy World. https://www.renewableenergyworld.com/2020/04/06/renewablesachieve- clean-energy-record-as-covid-19-hits-demand/, n.d. (accessed April 11, 2020)
Reusswig F, Braun F, Heger I et al (2016) Against the wind: local opposition to the German Energiewende. Util Policy 41(2016):214–227. https://doi.org/10.1016/j.jup.2016.02.006
Rifkin J (2011) The third industrial revolution: How lateral power is transforming energy, the economy, and the world. 1st edition. Palgrave Macmillan, New York, p 304
Sadorsky P (2009) Renewable energy consumption and income in emerging economies. Energy Policy 37(10):4021–4028. https://doi.org/10.1016/j.enpol.2009.05.003
Saenz DMG, Gonzalez PDR, Ignacio V (2008) Analysing the impact of renewable electricity support schemes on power prices: the case of wind electricity in Spain. Energy Policy 36(9):3345–3359. https://doi.org/10.1016/j.enpol.2008.04.022
Sapkota A, Lu Z, Yang H, Wang J (2014) Role of renewable energy technologies in rural communities' adaptation to climate change in Nepal. Renew Energy 68:793–800. https://doi.org/10.1016/j.renene.2014.03.003
Sastresa EL, Uson AA, Ignacio ZB, Scarpellini S (2010) Local impact of renewables on employment: assessment methodology and case study. Renew Sustain Energy Rev 14(2):679–690. https://doi.org/10.1016/j.rser.2009.10.017
Shafiei S, Salim RA (2014) Non-renewable and renewable energy consumption and CO_2 emissions in OECD countries: a comparative analysis. Energy Policy 66:547–556. https://doi.org/10.1016/j.enpol.2013.10.064
Siegrist M, Cvetkovich G (2000) Perception of hazards: the role of social trust and knowledge. Risk Anal 20(2000):713–720. https://doi.org/10.1111/0272-4332.205064
Sjöberg L, Moen BE, Rundmo T (2020) Explaining risk perception: An evaluation of the psychometric paradigm in risk perception research, Rotunde No. 84, Norwegian University of Science and Technology, Department of Psychology, Trondheim, 2004. Available via: http://www.svt.ntnu.no/psy/Torbjorn.Rundmo/Psychometric_paradigm.pdf. Accessed 28 April 2020
Songsore E, Buzzelli M (2014) Social responses to wind energy development in Ontario: the influence of health risk perceptions and associated concerns. Energy Policy 69(2014):285–296. https://doi.org/10.1016/j.enpol.2014.01.048
Tomescu M, Moorkens I, Meinke-hubeny F et al (2017) Renewable energy in Europe—2017 Update: recent growth and knock-on effects, EEA Report No 23/ 2017, Publications Office of the European Union, Luxembourg (2017. Available via: https://doi.org/10.2800/313983
Tugcu CT, Ozturk I, Aslan A (2012) Renewable and non-renewable energy consumption and economic growth relationship revisited: evidence from G7 countries. Energy Eco 34(6):1942–1950. https://doi.org/10.1016/j.eneco.2012.08.021
Turyareeba P (1993) Mobilizing local financial resources-the case of Uganda. In Energy options for Africa
United Nations Environment Programme, Frankfurt School of Finance and Management et Bloomberg New Energy Finance (UNEP, BNEF and FS- UNEP) (2020) Global trends in renewable energy investment 2020. June, p 80. Available via: https://www.fs-unep-centre.org/wp-content/uploads/2020/06/GTR_2020.pdf
United Nations Environment Programme, Frankfurt School of Finance and Management et Bloomberg New Energy Finance (UNEP, FSFM and BNEF), (2012) Global trends in renewable energy investment 2012. June, p 82. Available via: http://fs-unep-centre.org/sites/default/files/publications/globaltrendsreport2012.pdf
United Nations Environment Programme, Frankfurt School of Finance and Management et Bloomberg New Energy Finance (UNEP, FSFM and BNEF) (2015) Global trends in renewable energy investment 2015, key findings. March, p 16. Available via: http://fs-unep-centre.org/sites/default/files/attachments/key_findings.pdf
United Nations Environment Programme, International Labour Organization, International Organisation of Employers and International Trade Union Confederation (UNEP, ILO, IOE and ITUC)

(2008) Green Jobs: Towards decent work in a sustainable low carbon world. World watch Institute, Washington DC, September, p 350. Available via: http://www.unep.org/PDF/UNEPGreenjobs_report08.pdf
Visschers VHM, Siegrist M (2014) Find the differences and the similarities: relating perceived benefits, perceived costs and protected values to acceptance of five energy technologies. J Environ Psychol 40(2014):117–130. https://doi.org/10.1016/j.jenvp.2014.05.007
Wadley DA, Han JH, Elliott PG (2019) Risk hidden in plain sight: explaining homeowner perceptions of electricity transmission infrastructure. Energy Policy 132(2019):744–753. https://doi.org/10.1016/j.enpol.2019.06.022
Wei M, Patadia S, Kammen DM (2010) Putting renewables and energy efficiency to work: How many jobs can the clean energy industry generate in the US? Energy Policy 38(2):919–931. https://doi.org/10.1016/j.enpol.2009.10.044
Yadoo A, Cruickshank H (2012) The role for low carbon electrification technologies in poverty reduction and climate change strategies: a focus on renewable energy mini-grids with case studies in Nepal, Peru and Kenya. Energy Policy 42:591–602. https://doi.org/10.1016/j.enpol.2011.12.029
Yu X, Qu H (2013) The role of China's renewable powers against climate change during the 12th Five-Year and until 2020
Yüksel I (2008) Global warming and renewable energy sources for sustainable development in Turkey. Renew Energy 33(4):802–812. https://doi.org/10.1016/j.renene.2007.05.040

Narjess Aloui has a Ph.D. in Marketing. She is an assistant professor at Carthage Business School in Tunisia. Current research areas emphasize the market orientation strategies, investment and decision-making process and the role of digital marketing.

Imen Sdiri has a Ph.D. in Marketing. She is an assistant professor at Carthage University, ISG Bizerte. Current research areas emphasize consumer attitudes, Marketing for seniors, and innovation.

Rafla Hchaichi is an assistant professor in Economics at University Tunis Carthage, Carthage business school, and affiliate at ESCTRA lab IHEC Carthage, Tunisia. She holds her Ph.D. in Economics from Faculty of Economics and Management of Tunis Manar and she has a master's in finance and economic development. She undertakes research on public governance particularly public economics, bureaucracy, public choice, as well as new public management and total quality management. Her research includes topics such as cryptocurrency, energy, environment, climate change, and commodity market.

The Impact of Regulations, Energy Prices and Economic Activity on the India's Electric Power Consumption: A Kalman Filter Application

Sahbi Farhani

Abstract This study presents an analysis of the time-varying GDP, FDI, exports and energy price elasticities of electric power consumption in India over the period 1978–2015, using the Kalman filter approach. The results show that GDP and the energy price are two of the main drivers of electric power consumption in India, while FDI and exports are found to play a less significant role since they are monopoly-driven and relatively low when compared to international standards. These findings imply that increases in energy prices in India might have a significant impact on electric power consumption in the short- and long-run. Furthermore, several changes in FDI and exports seem to have affected the sensitivity of electric power consumption during the period prior to regulations, which made individuals, businesses, and agencies more sensitive to energy costs. On the other hand, the period after regulation has been characterized by more stable and declining sensitivity of electric power consumption. Therefore, factors such as regulations and changes in the country's economic activities appear to have affected GDP, FDI, exports and energy price elasticities of electric power consumption in India.

Keywords Regulations · Energy prices · Economic activity · Electric power consumption · Kalman filter

S. Farhani (✉)
Assistant Professor, Department of Economics and Quantitative Methods, Higher Institute of Finance and Taxation of Sousse, University of Sousse, Sousse, Tunisia
e-mail: sahbi.farhani@isffs.u-sousse.tn

QUARG UR17ES26, ESCT, Campus University of Manouba, 2010 Manouba, Tunisia

S. Goutte et al. (eds.), *Advances in Managing Energy and Climate Risks*,
Lecture Notes in Energy 82, https://doi.org/10.1007/978-3-030-71403-1_4

1 Introduction

Over the last few decades, India has experienced a steady increase in economic growth, and in keeping with this rise in economic growth, the demand for electricity consumption has also risen. Since 1978, the India per capita GDP has grown nearly 8 times, and in commensurate this economic growth pattern, the per capita energy consumption has gone up by 4 times (Fig. 1).[1] This consumption of energy has been in the form of fossil fuel and renewable energy consumption. Only after economic liberalization of 1990, renewable energy consumption started gaining prominence in Indian economic scenario, as the existing fossil fuel based energy generation infrastructure was proving out to be inadequate for catering to the rising demand for energy (Sinha and Bhattacharya 2014). As on 2015, nearly 28% of India's electricity generation capacity pertains to the renewable power plants, whereas the rest 72% is generated fro with the traditional non-renewable and fossil fuel based power plants (World Bank 2016). As in 2015, India has more than 25% of global share in per capita electricity consumption.

This increase in electricity consumption has coexisted with the rise in energy demand. During the last fifteen years, the highest electricity consumption was seen in commercial electricity consumption, followed by residential, industrial, and agricultural electricity consumption (TERI 2017). The demand is likely to rise further, as India strives to eradicate the energy poverty issues by means of rural electrification, following the Rajiv Gandhi Grameen Vidyutikaran Yojana (RGGVY) scheme. This is likely to increase the productivity of the households, which will in turn get reflected in the rise in agricultural electricity demand, and the disposable income of the households. This rise in income level of the rural households will be reflected in better quality of life, and this improvement will further be manifested in the demand for electricity by households.

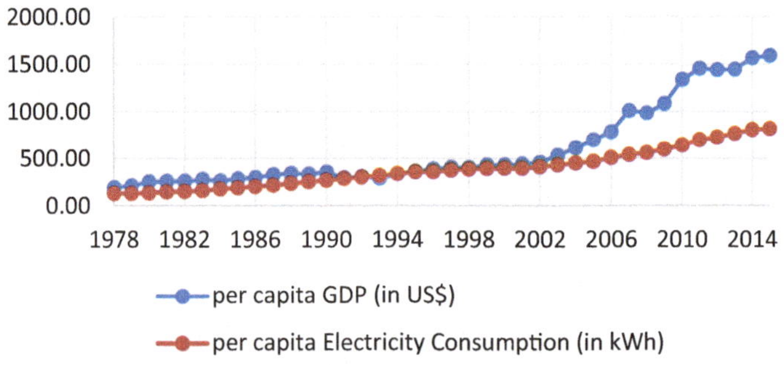

Fig. 1 Growth in per capita GDP viz-a-viz per capita electricity consumption in India

[1]World Development Indicators (World Bank 2016).

The existing fossil fuel based electricity generation infrastructure might not be able to cater for this demand escalation, and this problem is coexisting with the 13 Sustainable Development Goals (SDGs), which is focused at taking urgent action to combat climate change (United Nations 2015). In order to fulfill both of these objectives, India has gradually moving towards renewable energy sources for electricity production purpose (Sinha and Shahbaz 2018). These sources are majorly solar energy, wind energy, biomass energy, and hydroelectricity. As the renewable electricity production sources are gradually gaining prominence in Indian power production domain, they are able to attract both domestic and foreign investments. Foreign direct investments (FDIs) are expected from the International Finance Corporation (investment amount US$ 6 billion), GE Energy Financial Services (investment amount US$ 90 million), Greenko Energy Holdings (investment amount US$ 155 million), JERA Co. Inc (investment amount US$ 2 billion), and various other corporations (BP 2017). In order to complement this forthcoming FDI inflow, government is also taking up initiatives to boost the growth of renewable energy sources.

For example, (a) tariff of solar or wind electricity is planned to have a fixed-cost component (Ministry of New and Renewable Energy 2012), (b) solar power generation capacity will be increased by setting up more than fifty solar parks (Cabinet Committee on Economic Affairs 2017), (c) green energy corridor across states is planned, among many others (Ministry of New and Renewable Energy 2015). At the same time, government is also putting forth effort to boost the traditional fossil fuel based electricity generation mechanism, following a cleaner way. These initiatives include demolishing the monopoly of state-run coal mining firms by commercial auctioning of coal blocks, coal linkage by reverse auctioning, investment on advanced ultra-supercritical technologies for cleaner coal utilization, and various other (NITI Aayog2017).

Given this background, electricity generation is expected to be a crucial factor for India for catering to this demand, and thereby, maintaining the sustainability of economic growth. And in order to determine the nature of demand fluctuation, it is critical to understand the determinants of electricity production, and how demand is sensitive to these determinants. In this study, we have analyzed the energy price, GDP, FDI and exports elasticities of electric power demand in India over the period of 1978–2015. This paper contributes to the ongoing electricity debate, by analyzing the sensitivity of electricity demand in India, which is a potential and favorable investment destination for electricity generation. Following the works of Inglesi-Lotz (2011) for South Africa and Thamae et al. (2015) for Lesotho, we have used the Kalman filter approach to analyze the elasticity of the determinants of electricity demand. The results obtained from this study will help identify the areas, which need special attention for maintaining the balance between electricity demand and electricity supply in India.

The remainder of the paper is structured in the following manner. Section 2 presents a review of relevant literature, Sect. 3 introduces the econometric tools and data used in the study, Sect. 4 describes the results, Sect. 5 discusses the elasticities, and Sect. 6 concludes the study with relevant policy implications.

2 Studies on the Determinants of Electricity Demand

In the field of energy studies, determination of electricity demand always plays a significant role, as this has both economic and ecological consequences. This analysis gains more significance from the perspective of an emerging economy, within the context of SDGs. In this section, we will review the studies focusing on analyzing the determinants of electricity demand in various contexts.

Energy price is a factor, which has been identified as one of the predominant determinants of electricity demand by several researchers. Pouris (1987) analyzed the energy price elasticity of electricity demand for South Africa over the period of 1950–1983. Taking the unconstrained distributed lag model approach, the researcher found the long run elasticity to be −0.90. Al-Faris (2002) analyzed the energy price elasticity of residential electricity demand for GCC countries over the period of 1970–1997. Taking the Johansen (1991) cointegration approach, the researcher found the long run elasticity to be −1.68 and the short run elasticity to be −0.09. Holtedahl and Joutz (2004) analyzed the energy price elasticity of residential electricity demand for Taiwan over the period of 1955–1995. Taking the Engle and Granger (1987) cointegration and error-correction approach, the researchers found the both long run and short run elasticities to be −0.15. De Vita et al. (2006) analyzed the energy price elasticity of electricity demand for Namibia over the period of 1980–2002. By using autoregressive distributed lag (ARDL) and error correction model (ECM) approach, the researchers found the elasticity to be −0.34. Cho et al. (2007) analyzed the energy price elasticity of industrial electricity demand for South Korea over the period of 1991–2003. By using logistic diffusion approach, the researchers found the elasticity to be 0.04. Halicioglu (2007) analyzed the energy price elasticity of residential electricity demand for Turkey over the period of 1968–2005.

Taking the bounds test approach, the researcher found the long run elasticity to be −0.52 and the short run elasticity to be −0.33. Alberini and Filippini (2011) analyzed the energy price elasticity of residential electricity demand for 48 US states over the period of 1995–2007. Taking the (a) corrected Least Square Dummy Variables (LSDV) approach of Kiviet (1995), the researchers found the long run elasticity to be −0.43 and short run elasticity to be −0.14, and (b) System GMM approach of Blundell and Bond (2000), the researchers found the long run elasticity to be −0.73 and short run elasticity to be −0.15. A summary of the reviewed studies is provided in Table 1. Barring a few cases, it can be observed that the energy price elasticity of electricity demand is largely found to be negative. In Indian context, one of the foremost studies has been carried out by Filippini and Pachauri (2004), and this study found the long run elasticity ranging between −0.51 and −0.29. However, this study was carried out over the period of 1993–1994, and that was when industrialization in India started gaining pace after economic liberalization. Given the period considered in the present study, the Indian economic scenario has undergone a transformation owing to a number of socio-political factors, and that is why, it is needed to analyze this energy price elasticity of electricity demand in India.

Table 1 Summary of reviewed studies

Author(s)	Country	Period	Methodology	Result
Energy price elasticity				
Pouris (1987)	South Africa	1950–1983	Unconstrained distributed lag model	Long run: −0.90 Short run: NA
Al-Faris (2002)	GCC countries	1970–1997	Johansen co-integration	Long run: −1.68 Short run: −0.09
Filippini and Pachauri (2004)	India	1993–1994	OLS	Long run: between −0.51 and −0.29
Holtedahl and Joutz (2004)	Taiwan	1955–1995	Engle and Granger (1987)	Long run: −0.15 Short run: −0.15
De Vita et al. (2006)	Namibia	1980–2002	ARDL and ECM	Long run: −0.34
Cho et al. (2007)	South Korea	1991–2003	Logistic diffusion	0.04
Halicioglu (2007)	Turkey	1968–2005	Bound test	Long run: −0.52 Short run: −0.33
Alberini and Filippini (2011)	48 US states	1995–2007	Kiviet corrected LSDV (1995)	Long run: −0.43 Short run: −0.14
			Blundell-Bond GMM (1998)	Long run: −0.73 Short run: −0.15
Income elasticity				
Ibrahim and Hurst (1990)	Brazil	1970 to mid-1980s	OLS	Long run: 1.16
	India			Long run: 1.56
	Korea			Long run: 1.22
	Morocco			Long run: 1.03
	Pakistan			Long run: 1.33
	Philippines			Long run: 1.14
	Taiwan			Long run: 1.24
	Thailand			Long run: 1.08
	Algeria			Long run: 0.89
	Egypt			Long run: 0.85
	Indonesia			Long run: 1.19
	Mexico			Long run: 1.27
	Saudi Arabia			Long run: 1.23
Balabanoff (1994)	Argentina	1970–1990	OLS	Long run: 1.00
	Brazil			Long run: 1.93
	Chile			Long run: 1.65
	Columbia			Long run: 1.88
	Ecuador			Long run: 1.95

(continued)

Table 1 (continued)

Author(s)	Country	Period	Methodology	Result
	Mexico			Long run: 0.69
	Peru			Long run: 0.70
	Venezuela			Long run: NA
Hunt et al. (1999)	Honduras	1973–1995	Cointegration	Long run: 0.79
Filippini and Pachauri (2004)	India	1993–1994	OLS	Long run: between 0.60 and 0.64
Jumbe (2004)	Malawi	1970–1999	ECM	Long run: 0.25
De Vita et al. (2006)	Namibia	1980–2002	ARDL and ECM	Long run: 1.27
Bianco et al. (2009)	Italy	1970–2007	Multiple regression	Long run: between 0.29 and 1.41
FDI elasticity				
Bekhet and bt Othman (2011)	Malaysia	1971–2009	ECM	Long run: −0.18
Bento (2011)	Portugal	1980–2007	ARDL	Long run: −0.04 Short run: −0.01
Shahbaz et al. (2011)	Portugal	1971–2009	VECM	Long run: 0.04
Zaman et al. (2012)	Pakistan	1975–2010	ARDL	Long run: 0.06 Short run: 0.03
Sbia et al. (2014)	The UAE	1975–2011	ARDL	Long run: −0.06 Short run: −0.02
Keho (2016)	Benin	1970–2011	ARDL	Long run: −0.02
	Cameroon			Long run: 0.03
	Congo Rep.			Long run: 0.01
	Congo DR			Long run: −0.01
	Côte d'Ivoire			Long run: −0.02
	Gabon			Long run: 0.01
	Ghana			Long run: −0.02
	Kenya			Long run: 0.04
	Nigeria			Long run: −0.02
	Senegal			Long run: −0.07
	South Africa			Long run: −0.04
	Togo			Long run: −0.01
Trade elasticity				
Cole (2006)	32 countries	1975–1995	OLS	Long run: 1.47

Apart from the energy price, GDP is also considered as one of the critical determinants of electricity demand. The demand for electricity rises with the level of industrialization, which is a reflection of the GDP or income growth. Researchers have analyzed this association in several contexts. One of the earliest studies in this context was carried out by Ibrahim and Hurst (1990). The researchers analyzed the pattern of energy demand in developing countries between the period of 1970 and mid-1980s. The income elasticities of the countries found to be within the range of 0.85 and 1.56. In a subsequent study, Balabanoff (1994) analyzed the electricity demand for eight Latin American countries over the period of 1970–1990. The income elasticities of the countries found to be within the range of 0.69 and 1.95. Hunt et al. (1999) analyzed the income elasticity of electricity generation for Honduras over the period of 1973–1995. The researchers found the long run elasticity to be 0.79. Jumbe (2004) analyzed the income elasticity of electricity demand for Malawi over the period of 1970–1999. Taking the ECM approach, the researcher found the long run elasticity to be 0.25. De Vita et al. (2006) analyzed the income elasticity of electricity demand for Namibia over the period of 1980–2002. By using ARDL and ECM approach, the researchers found the elasticity to be 1.27. Bianco et al. (2009) analyzed the income elasticity of electricity demand for Italy over the period of 1970–2007. Taking the multiple regression approach, the researcher found the long run elasticity to be between 0.29 and 1.41. A summary of the reviewed studies is provided in Table 1. Looking at the results of the reviewed studies, it can be observed that the income elasticity of electricity demand is largely found to be positive. In Indian context, one of the foremost studies has been carried out by Filippini and Pachauri (2004), and this study found the long run elasticity ranging between 0.60 and 0.64. However, this study was carried out over the period of 1993–1994, and that was when India started experiencing the transition from manufacturing-driven economy to a service economy. Given the period considered in the present study, the Indian economic scenario has undergone a transformation owing to a number of global economic factors, and that is why, it is needed to analyze this income elasticity of electricity demand in India.

In keeping with the growth in industrialization and income, the foreign direct investments (FDI) and trade rise. These investments add to the level of industrialization, and thereby rise in income. Growth in both industrialization and income by means of FDI and trade entail rise in the demand of electricity. This rise in electricity demand can be experienced both at the industrial and residential level. Researchers have identified this association between FDI and electricity demand in several contexts. Bekhet and bt Othman (2011) analyzed the determinants of electricity demand for Malaysia over the period of 1971–2009. Following the ECM approach, the researchers found the long run FDI elasticity of electricity demand to be −0.18. Bento (2011) analyzed the impact of FDI on energy savings for Portugal over the period of 1980–2007. Following the ARDL approach, the researcher found the long run FDI elasticity of electricity consumption to be −0.04 and short run elasticity to be −0.01. However, this result for Portugal has been contradicted by Shahbaz et al. (2011). Zaman et al. (2012) analyzed the determinants of electricity consumption function in Pakistan over the period of 1975–2010. Following the ARDL bounds approach, the researchers found the long run FDI elasticity of electricity consumption to be 0.06 and short run elasticity to be 0.03. Sbia et al. (2014) analyzed the contributing factors of electricity demand in the UAE during the period of 1975–2011. The researchers found both the long run and short run elasticities to be −0.02.

Apart from these studies, researchers have largely considered electricity consumption as a measurable proxy for electricity demand. In a recent study, Keho (2016) analyzed the drivers of energy consumption in 12 African countries over the period of 1970–2011. Following ARDL approach, the long run FDI elasticity of electricity consumption found to be between −0.07 and 0.04. Through the review of these studies, the impact of FDI on electricity consumption or demand is found to be inconclusive. This can be attributed to the level of development in the nations, the nature of technology transfer by means of FDI, and the energy intensity achieved through the technological innovation catalyzed by FDI inflow. As India is moving forward to attain the SDG objectives largely through clean energy processes, and a huge amount of FDI is being channeled to achieve that purpose, it is imperative to assess the impact of FDI on electricity demand.

Researchers have also identified the association between trade and electricity demand in several contexts. As an example, Cole (2006) analyzed the impact of trade liberalization on energy use for 32 developing and developed countries over the period of 1975–1995. Following a fixed effect regression approach, the researcher found the long run elasticity of trade intensity with respect to per capita energy use is 1.47.

As a whole, through this review of literature, we have understood the importance of including energy price, GDP, FDI, and trade to assess the electricity demand in India. The reviewed studies comply with our model specification, by addressing the gap in the literature.

3 Method and Materials

3.1 General Issues

Prior to applying Kalman filter technique, we first proposed four unit root tests that we will apply to test the unit root properties of each series of variables. These tests are ADF of Dickey and Fuller (1979), PP of Phillips and Perron (1988) and Zivot-Andrews of Zivot and Andrews (1992) unit root tests. Then we mention that since the testing procedures for ADF and PP are well known, we will not limit to them here, but we will add some spaces for another more important test. This is due to that the study period is characterized by major changes in the global landscape which can potentially cause structural breaks. In fact, ADF and PP are the commonly used unit root tests to find out the order of integration of a variable. Therefore, attempts have been made to develop test of unit root which incorporates presence of structural breaks in the null of unit root hypothesis. At this level, we will apply the Zivot-Andrews unit root test to identify single unknown structural break arising in the series.

In addition, empirical modelling has essentially characterized the last three decades with co-integration analysis being one of the main econometric developments (Engle and Granger 1987; Johansen 1991; Hendry and Juselius 2000, 2001). Energy and its determinants related econometric analysis were not the exception of the trend. Although popular, the co-integration approaches are profoundly relying on the stationarity of the series and also on the hypothesis that the estimated parameters are fairly stable over time (the averages of the estimated coefficients are used throughout this study). Given these claims, researchers have started thinking with suspicious to the overdependence on the co-integration analysis in some cases. For this reason, Harvey (1997) has studied the case and finds that all dynamic econometrics should not be revolved around autoregressive modelling. Also Hunt et al. (2003) added that methodologies that use regression models with stochastically varying coefficients allow over time have already been proven to be very effective. The Kalman filter methodology that this paper uses show all the above-mentioned characteristics and hands over the ideal frame for estimating regressions with variables whose impacts change over time (Slade 1989). Morrison and Pike (1977) also mention that on condition where the estimated coefficients do not change over time, the Kalman filter and the least squares approach beseem to conclude similar results. However in the presence of parameter instability, the Kalman filter can be proven superior to the least squares model (Morrison and Pike 1977). Therefore, before choosing the most appropriate technique for a specific case, the researcher needs to establish the possibility of existing parameter instability. To test for instability of parameters, a number of tests are proposed in the literature (Chu 1989; Hansen 1992; Andrews 1993). Hansen (1997) proposes an extended version of past approaches to cover general models with stochastic and deterministic trends. The null hypothesis is parameter stability and he proposes use of the "Sup" test of Quandt and the "Exp" and "Ave" tests of Andrews and Ploberger (1994). Performing this test in this paper will confirm or reject the assumption of time-varying regressors elasticities, before estimating them. If the estimated coefficients are proven to vary over time, then the Kalman filter is the most appropriate method.

In addition, the Kalman filter is characterized as predictive and adaptive because it looks forward with an estimate of the covariance and mean of the time series one step into the future. What makes it efficient is that as a recursive filter, it estimates the internal state of a linear dynamic system from a series of noisy measurements. The Kalman filter can be considered to be one of the simplest dynamic Bayesian networks (Masreliez and Martin 1977). The Kalman filter calculates estimates of the true values of measurements recursively over time using incoming measurements and a mathematical process model. Next, the Kalman filter application is presented thoroughly.

3.2 Kalman Filter Application

The Kalman filter technique is based on the estimation of state-space models that were originally employed for engineering and chemistry applications (Wiener 1949; Kalman 1960, 1963). Researchers started applying the technique in economics only in the 1980s (Lawson 1980; Harvey 1987; Cuthbertson 1988; Milani 2007). According to Cuthbertson et al. (1993), there are two main types of models in compliance to representation via Kalman filter: (a) unobservable components models and (b) time-varying parameter models.

Firstly, the formal representation of a dynamic system written in state-space form suitable for the Kalman filter should be described. The following system of equations presents the state-space model of the dynamics of a $(n \times 1)$ vector, y_t.

$$\text{Observation equation}: \quad y_t = Ax_t + B\rho_t + \mu_t \tag{1}$$

$$\text{State equation}: \quad \rho_{t+1} = C\rho_t + \eta_{t+1} \tag{2}$$

where A, B and C are matrices of parameters of dimension $(n \times k)$, $(n \times r)$ and $(r \times r)$, respectively, and x_t is a $(k \times 1)$ vector of exogenous or predetermined variables, ρ_t is a $(r \times 1)$ vector of possibly unobserved state variables, known as the state vector. The following two equations represent the characteristics of the disturbance vectors μ_t and η_t, which are assumed to be independent white noise.

$$E\left(\eta_t\eta_t^{'}\right) = \begin{cases} Q & for\, t = \tau \\ 0 & otherwise \end{cases}; \quad E\left(\mu_t\mu_t^{'}\right) = \begin{cases} R & for\, t = \tau \\ 0 & otherwise \end{cases} \tag{3}$$

where Q and R are $(r \times r)$ and $(n \times n)$ matrices, respectively. As shown in the following two equations, the disturbances η_t and μ_t are uncorrelated at all lags.

$$E\left(\eta_t\mu_t^{'}\right) = 0 \quad \text{for all } t \text{ and } \tau \tag{4}$$

In the observation equation the factor x_t is considered to be predetermined or exogenous which does not provide information about ρ_{t+s} or μ_{t+s} for $s = 0, 1, 2, \ldots$ beyond what is given by the sequence $y_{t-1}, y_{t-2}, \ldots$. Thus, x_t could include lagged values of y or variables which are uncorrelated with ρ_t and μ_t for all τ. The overall system of equations is used to explain a finite series of observations $\{y_1, y_2, \ldots, y_T\}$ for which assumptions about the initial value of the state vector ρ_t are needed. The assumption that the parameter matrices (A, B, C, Q or R) are functions of time, the state-space representation Eqs. (1) and (2) becomes:

$$y_t = \alpha(x_t) + B(x_t)\rho_t + \mu_t \tag{5}$$

$$\rho_{t+1} = C(x_t)\rho_t + \eta_{t+1} \tag{6}$$

where $C(x_t)$ is a $(r \times r)$ matrix whose elements are functions of x_t, $\alpha(x_t)$ is a $(n \times 1)$ vector-valued function and $B(x_t)$ is a $(n \times r)$ matrix-valued function.

Equations (5) and (6) allow for stochastically varying parameters, but are more restrictive in the sense that a Gaussian distribution is assumed.

3.3 Theoretical Model

In the past, local and international models primarily assumed that the price elasticity of electricity remained constant over time. However, electricity models have to allow price sensitivity to change over time in order to capture the changes in economic conditions as well as developments in the electricity market (Inglesi-Lotz 2011). Equations (7–8) include standard variables, used in international and local literature (Inglesi 2010; Nakajima and Hamori 2010; Dilaver and Hunt 2011) such as prices of electricity and output of the economy, to explain the electricity consumption.

$$\ln EPC_t = \alpha \ln GDP_t + \beta FDI_t + \gamma \ln EX_t + \delta \ln WPI_t + \varepsilon_t \tag{7}$$

where *EPC* is the electric power consumption; *GDP* is the gross domestic product of the economy; *FDI* is the foreign direct investment; *EX* is the exports of goods and services; and *WPI* is the price of electric power consumption. All variables are in their natural logs, as indicated, except *FDI*.

The estimation of this equation would result in a constant coefficient α representing the income elasticity of electric power consumption; a constant coefficient β representing the investment elasticity of electric power consumption; a constant coefficient γ representing the exports elasticity of electric power consumption and a constant coefficient δ representing the price elasticity of electric power consumption. However, in this study by applying a Kalman filter estimation, the coefficients α, β, γ and δ are time varying; hence, the equation to be estimated looks as follows:

$$\ln EPC_t = \alpha_t \ln GDP_t + \beta_t FDI_t + \gamma_t \ln EX_t + \delta_t \ln WPI_t + \varepsilon_t \tag{8}$$

We estimate the following model which contains six equations allowing for time-varying coefficients:

$$\ln EPC_t = sv_1 \ln GDP_t + sv_2 FDI_t + sv_3 \ln EX_t + sv_4 \ln WPI_t + sv_5 \tag{9}$$

$$sv_1 = sv_1(-1) \tag{10}$$

$$sv_2 = sv_2(-1) \tag{11}$$

$$sv_3 = sv_3(-1) \tag{12}$$

$$sv_4 = sv_4(-1) \quad (13)$$

$$sv_5 = c(2)sv_5(-1) + [\text{var} = \exp(c(1))] \quad (14)$$

Equations (10–13) show that the time varying coefficients evolve through time according to a random walk process. All variables are integrated of order 1, I(1).

3.4 Data

To apply the Kalman filter techniques for the analysis, local and international sources of data were used. All data are obtained from an online database of World Bank with annual observation spanning from 1978–2015. Energy consumption is measured as Electric Power Consumption (EPC) (kWh per capita), GDP per capita (constant 2005 US$), Foreign Direct Investment (FDI)—net inflows (constant 2005 US$ per capita), Exports (EX) is measured by Exports of goods and services (constant 2005 US$ per capita), and Whole-sale Price Index (WPI) is used as proxy for energy prices.

Table 2 summarizes the descriptive statistics of the series (in their linearised version and the difference of the linear). These elementary descriptive statistics (in their majority, averages through the period) are reported only as an indication of the nature of the raw data to be used in the analysis.

Figure 2 presents Plots in natural logarithm of Electric power consumption (EPC), GDP per capita, Foreign direct investment (FDI), Exports of goods and services (EX), and Energy prices (WPI) for 1978–2015 in India. The overall positive relationship

Table 2 Descriptive statistics over the period of 1978–2015

	ln*EPC*	ln*GDP*	*FDI*	ln*EX*	ln*WPI*
Mean	5.835912	6.607557	0.091183	4.378552	3.770848
Median	5.910562	6.538804	0.053348	4.181648	3.902120
Maximum	6.745236	7.498870	0.450272	6.073157	4.867260
Minimum	4.912655	5.966147	0.000549	3.196255	2.357935
Std. Dev.	0.536906	0.462793	0.111076	1.002990	0.736536
Skewness	−0.149087	0.405191	1.466868	0.360826	−0.243111
Kurtosis	2.043360	1.938742	4.453702	1.629119	1.882094
Jarque-Bera	1.589773	2.823061	16.97342	3.800154	2.353031
Probability	0.451632	0.243770	0.000206	0.149557	0.308351
Sum	221.7647	251.0872	3.464956	166.3850	143.2922
Sum Sq. Dev.	10.66592	7.924579	0.456500	37.22159	20.07198
Observations	38	38	38	38	38

[a]Std. Dev. indicates standard deviation

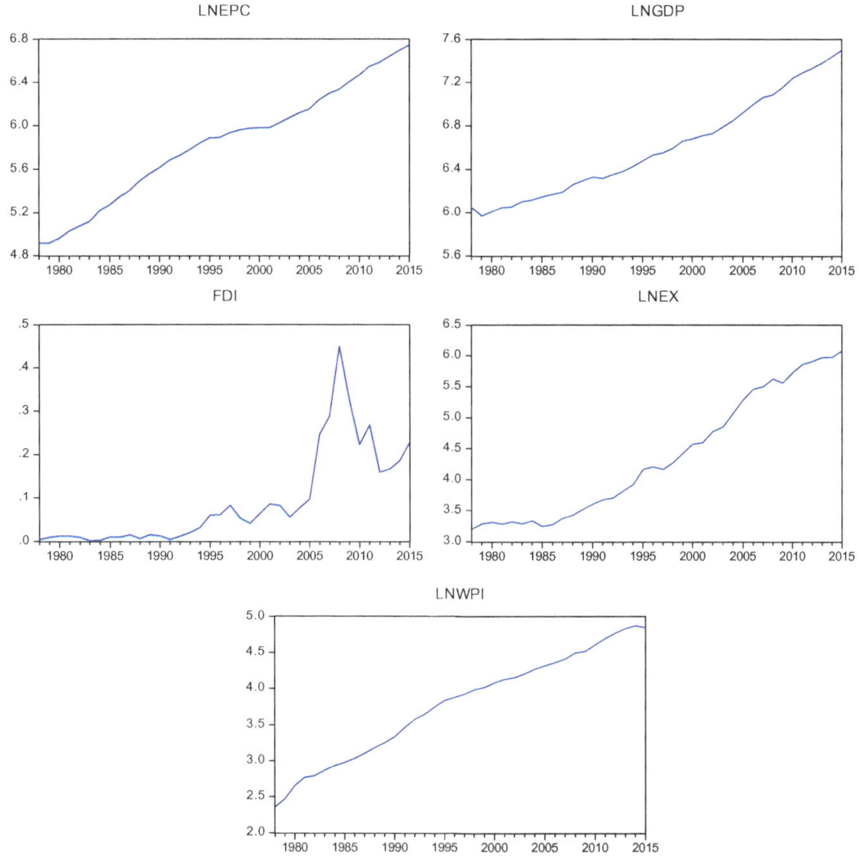

Fig. 2 Plots in natural logarithm of Electric power consumption (EPC), GDP, Foreign direct investment (FDI), Exports of goods and services (EX), and Energy prices (WPI) for 1978–2015 in India

between WPI and EPC is observable from this figure, since both the WPI and EPC show a clear upward trend through the years of the present period. This result seems to contradict with Inglesi-Lotz (2011) who worked on the case of South Africa as an African country. Similarly, the relationship between EPC and GDP is also shown to be positive, since both of them show an upward trend for the time period in question. This result seems to support Inglesi-Lotz (2011).

4 Empirical Results

As discussed in the methodology section, before applying the Kalman filter, we have applied ADF, PP and Zivot-Andrews unit root tests to examine the integrating properties of the variables. The results of all tests reported in Tables 3 and 4 reveal

Table 3 Unit root tests results

	(With intercept and trend)		(Only with intercept)	
	ADF			
	Level	Δ	Level	Δ
ln*EPC*	−1.0878 (0.9176)	−4.5246[a] (0.0058)	−0.3082 (0.9141)	−4.5267[a] (0.0009)
ln*GDP*	−2.2144 (0.4680)	−2.960[a] (0.0090)	3.3394 (1.0000)	−6.8251[a] (0.0000)
FDI	−2.4150 (0.3662)	−5.8173[a] (0.0002)	−1.2593 (0.6379)	−5.8951[a] (0.0000)
ln*EX*	−2.2665 (0.4408)	−5.3904[a] (0.0005)	1.4178 (0.9987)	−4.9182[a] (0.0003)
ln*WPI*	−1.8163 (0.6764)	−3.7193[b] (0.0337)	−1.3305 (0.6405)	−3.1040[b] (0.0352)
	PP			
ln*EPC*	−1.5855 (0.7795)	−4.5934[a] (0.0040)	−0.3201 (0.9122)	−4.6173[a] (0.0007)
ln*GDP*	−2.2202 (0.4649)	−12.365[a] (0.0000)	4.7706 (1.0000)	−6.6442[a] (0.0000)
FDI	−2.4969 (0.3278)	−5.8174[a] (0.0002)	−1.2816 (0.6278)	−5.8952[a] (0.0000)
ln*EX*	−2.2852 (0.4311)	−5.4048[a] (0.0005)	1.4178 (0.9987)	−4.9074[a] (0.0003)
ln*WPI*	−1.9623 (0.6020)	−3.7261[b] (0.0332)	−1.0831 (0.9005)	−2.8065[c] (0.0673)

Note Δ is the first difference term. The tests ADF of Dickey and Fuller (1979) and PP of Phillips and Perron (1988) examine the null hypothesis of non-stationary. For ADF, the optimal lag length stands for the lag level that maximizes the Schwarz Information Criteria (SIC). For PP, Barlett Kernel is used as the spectral estimation method. The bandwidth is selected using the Newey–West method

P-values are in parentheses and report underneath the corresponding t-statistics

a, *b* and *c* indicate significance at 1, 5 and 10% levels, respectively

Table 4 Zivot–Andrews structural break unit root test results

	At level		At first difference	
	T-statistics	Time break	T-statistics	Time break
ln*EPC*	−1.8260(5)	2003	−5.2343 * (1)	2001
ln*GDP*	−0.4926 (1)	2003	−9.1244 * (1)	1989
FDI	0.5032 (3)	2005	−6.2076 * (4)	2001
ln*EX*	−0.3062(1)	1993	−5.8990 * (1)	1990
ln*WPI*	−0.4911 (1)	1990	−2.2057 ** (1)	2002

Note Lag length of variables is shown in small parentheses

* and ** indicate significance at 1% and 5% level, respectively

Table 5 Hansen test results for parameter stability: Quandt-Andrews unknown breakpoint test (Null hypothesis: No breakpoints within 15% trimmed data)

Statistic	Value	Prob.
Sup LR F-statistic	8.9303	0.0000
Sup Wald F-statistic	44.651	0.0000
Exp LR F-statistic	2.6196	0.0001
Exp Wald F-statistic	19.067	0.0000
Ave LR F-statistic	3.6260	0.0001
Ave Wald F-statistic	18.130	0.0001

Note Probabilities calculated using Hansen's (1997) method

that all series appear to have a unit root in their levels, while they are stationary in their first differences form. Thus, we conclude that all variables are integrated of order one, i.e. $I(1)$.

The Hansen test will assist by confirming whether the estimated parameters change over time. The null hypothesis of the test is that the parameters are stable; contrary to the alternative that indicates parameter instability. The results are displayed in Table 5.

The F-statistics of Quandt are 8.9303 with p-value of 0.0000 for Sup likelihood ratio (LR) and 44.651 with p-value of 0.0000 for Sup Wald. The F-statistics of Andrews and Ploberger (1994) for Exp LR, Exp Wald, Ave LR and Ave Wald are 2.6196 (p-value of 0.0001), 19.067 (p-value of 0.0000), 3.6260 (p-value of 0.0001) and 18.130 (p-value of 0.0001), respectively. Since the p-values are smaller than the 10% level of significance, the Hansen test does reject the null hypothesis that the parameters are stable. Given this result we proceed with the Kalman filter application. Although, our study focuses on the evolution of energy price elasticity of electric power consumption, the model allows us to observe the evolution of GDP, FDI and exports elasticities for the same period.

Table 6 reports the Kalman filter estimation results. $c(1)$ and $c(2)$ represent the constant parameters of the estimation; sv_1, sv_2, sv_3 and sv_4 represent the final estimates for GDP, FDI, exports and energy priceelasticities, respectively; and sv_5 the value of the rest of the factors affecting the dependent variable (electric power consumption).

The final (average) estimates of the Kalman filter estimation technique for: (i) GDP and energy price elasticities being significant and having the values of 0.291242 (0.0501) and 0.187873 (0.0407), respectively; and (ii) FDI and exports elasticities being no significant and having the values of 0.048033 (0.5456) and −0.054322 (0.2735), respectively. These show that, on average, increases in energy price have resulted in more than proportionate rise in electric power consumption, implying that the demand for electric power consumption in India is price elastic. This could be expected given the monopolistic nature of the country's electricity sector as well as the relatively high electricity prices when compared to international standards. Thus, increases in energy prices in India might have a significant impact on consumption in

Table 6 Kalman filter estimation results

Space model		
Method	Maximum likelihood (Marquardt)	
Sample	1978–2015	
Included observations	38	
Number of iterations to convergence	11	
Variables	*Estimated Coefficient*	*Prob.*
C(1)	−7.479349	0.0000
C(2)	1.008474	0.0000
	Final State	*Prob.*
sv1(dlnGDP)	0.291242	0.0501
sv2(dfdi)	0.048033	0.5456
sv3(dlnex)	−0.054322	0.2735
sv4(dlnwpi)	0.187873	0.0407
sv5(constant)	4.004628	0.0045
Goodness of fit		
Log likelihood	42.31197	
Akaike info criterion	−2.121682	
Schwarz criterion	−2.035494	
Hannan-Quinn criterion	−2.091017	

the short-run. However, if the energy prices become too high over time, consumers might change their behavior and sensitivity to price and hence, energy policymakers will need to reconsider their impact in the long-run (Thamae et al. 2015).

On the other hand, these findings reveal that the electric power consumption in India is GDP elastic. This is because the effect of a rise in the country's national GDP has generally produced a more than proportionate increase in electric power consumption. Therefore, economic growth seems to have been one of the main drivers of electric power consumption in India. Nevertheless, this study focuses on the evolution of GDP and energy price elasticities of electric power consumption (Thamae et al. 2015).

5 Discussion

After confirming with Hansen's test that the elasticities (time varying parameters) did indeed change over time for the studied period, the finding of the Kalman filter showed the evolution of the GDP, FDI, exports and energy price elasticities through the last three decades (Fig. 3).

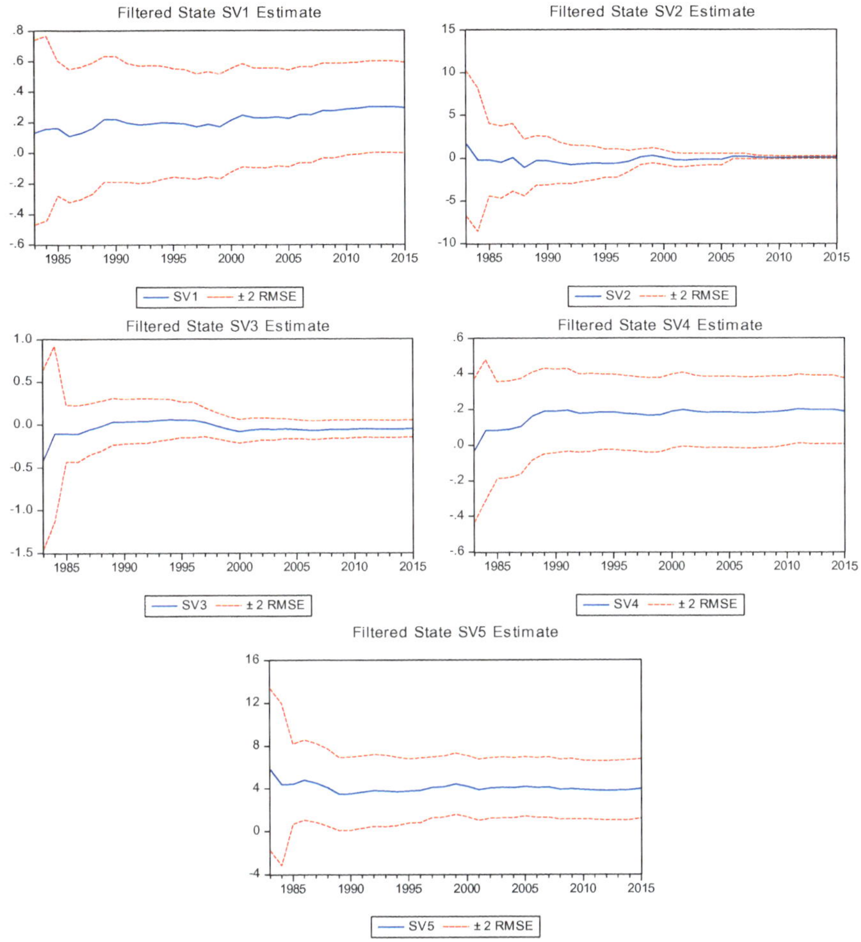

Fig. 3 Plots of Kalman filtered state estimates

It is found that: (i) the effect of GDP (sv1) to electric power consumption is more significant of increased values from 1.5 in 1983 to almost 2 unit elastic in 2015; (ii) the effect of FDI to electric power consumption starts with 1.5 unit elastic in 1983 and almost shows a small decrease in 1984 before to know a stable form which closes to zero at the end of the period; (iii) the effect of exports to electric power consumption shows a simple increase between 1983 and 1984 (from −0.4 to −0.1) after that a stable form is presented until which closes to −0.1 at the end of the period; (iv) similarly, the price elasticity present a huge increase during the period 1983–1989 (from −0.02 in 1983 to almost 2 in 1989), however, since then, it has become less significant and show a stable form which closes to almost 1.8 at the end of the period.

6 Conclusion and Policy Implications

This study provides an empirical analysis of the time-varying GDP, FDI, exports and energy price elasticities of electric power consumption in India for the period 1978–2015 using the Kalman filter approach. The results show that GDP and energy price are two of the main drivers of electric power consumption in India while FDI and exports are found to play a less significant role since they are monopoly-driven and relatively low when compared to international standards. This implies that increases in energy price in India might have a significant impact on electric power consumption in the short- and long-run.

The analysis of the price elasticity of electricity is not a recent topic in the continuous debate on energy economics of the last decade. Especially, in South Africa the effect of electricity prices to the electricity consumption is of high importance for the energy policy makers after the recurring price hikes applied by Eskom and approved by NERSA. Our paper's contribution to the existing international and local literature is the argument that the price elasticity is a time varying indicator. It changes over time due to a number of reasons such as the economic activity and its importance, the regulation of prices and the level of prices. We used the Kalman filter to model our assumption of time varying coefficients of price and income with regards to electricity consumption. This technique was preferred for a number of reasons. Firstly, it allows for the components to vary stochastically over time. It is a predictive and adaptive as well as it can be used with non-stationary data. For these reasons, it provides the ideal framework for estimating equation with variables that their impact varies over time. International and local studies estimated the price elasticity of aggregate (but also residential) electricity within the range of 2–0 and income elasticity between 0 and 2 (Inglesi 2010; Nakajima and Hamori 2010).

Thus, it is of high importance to mention that our results for the price and income elasticities are within the previously estimated ranges. The results show a decreasing effect of electricity prices to electricity consumption during the period examined. This decreasing trend is in contrast with the increasing income elasticity for the same period. An interesting additional finding is that the higher the prices (for example in the 1980s), the higher the price sensitivity of the consumers to changes in prices, that is the price elasticity of electricity is higher for higher levels of real prices. These results are of great significance for the energy policy makers of the country. NERSA's recent decisions, after Eskom's applications, will lead to higher prices and finally, to pricing structures similar to the 1980s. Initially the first price increases might not affect the electricity consumption significantly and directly since, the price elasticity is close to zero. However, if the real prices return to the high levels (close or higher to the levels of the 1980s), the energy policy makers need to reconsider the impact of prices in the long-run. Further increases of the electricity prices may lead to changes in the behaviour of electricity consumers and their sensitivity to prices. By focusing their efforts on improving their efficiency levels, the electricity consumers may introduce demand-side management techniques or even turn to other sources of—cheaper—energy, in order to "avoid" the high cost of electricity usage.

Future research would be focused on the investigation of whether the proposed relationship between real prices of electricity and price elasticity holds for other developed and developing countries. It would be of interest also to examine the evolution of income elasticity for other countries. Attention should be paid to cases of countries for which past studies concluded that there is no impact of electricity prices to electricity consumption for certain periods.

References

Aayog NITI (2017) Energizing India: a joint project report of NITI Aayog and IEEJ. National Institution for Transforming India, New Delhi

Alberini A, Filippini M (2011) Response of residential electricity demand to price: the effect of measurement error. Energy Econ 33:889–895

Al-Faris ARF (2002) The demand for electricity in the GCC countries. Energy Policy 30:117–124

Andrews DWK (1993) Tests for parameter instability and structural change with unknown change point. Econom 61:821–856

Andrews DWK, Ploberger W (1994) Optimal tests when a nuisance parameter is present only under the alternative. Econom 62:1383–1414

Balabanoff S (1994) The dynamics of energy demand in Latin America. OPEC Energy Rev 18:467–488

Bekhet HA, bt Othman NS (2011) Causality analysis among electricity consumption, consumer expenditure, gross domestic product (GDP) and foreign direct investment (FDI): Case study of Malaysia. J Econ Int Financ 3:228–235

Bento JP (2011) Energy savings via foreign direct investment: empirical evidence from Portugal. Working Paper No. 2011/24, Maastricht School of Management

Bianco V, Manca O, Nardini S (2009) Electricity consumption forecasting in Italy using linear regression models. Energy 34:1413–1421

Blundell R, Bond S (2000) GMM estimation with persistent panel data: an application to production functions. Econom Rev 19:321–340

BP (2017) BP statistical review of world energy 2017

Cabinet Committee on Economic Affairs (2017) Cabinet approves enhancement of capacity from 20,000 MW to 40,000 MW of the scheme for development of solar parks and ultra mega solar power projects. Press Information Bureau, Government of India

Cho Y, Lee J, Kim TY (2007) The impact of ICT investment and energy price on industrial electricity demand: Dynamic growth model approach. Energy Policy 35:4730–4738

Chu C-SJ (1989) New tests for parameter constancy in stationary and non-stationary regression models. University of California at San Diego, Mimeo

Cole MA (2006) Does trade liberalization increase national energy use? Econ Lett 92:108–112

Cuthbertson K (1988) Expectations, learning and the Kalman filter. Manch Sch 56:223–246

Cuthbertson K, Hall SG, Taylor MP (1993) Applied econometric techniques. University of Michigan Press, USA

De Vita G, Endresen K, Hunt LC (2006) An empirical analysis of energy demand in Namibia. Energy Policy 34:3447–3463

Dickey DA, Fuller WA (1979) Distribution of the estimators for autoregressive time series with unit root. J Am Stat Assoc 74:427–431

Dilaver Z, Hunt LC (2011) Industrial electricity demand for Turkey: A structural time series analysis. Energy Econ 33:426–436

Engle RF, Granger CWJ (1987) Co-integration and error correction: representation, estimation, and testing. Econom 55:251–276

Filippini M, Pachauri S (2004) Elasticities of electricity demand in urban Indian households. Energy Policy 32:429–436
Halicioglu F (2007) Residential electricity demand dynamics in Turkey. Energy Econ 29:199–210
Hansen BE (1992) Tests for parameter instability in regressions with I(1) processes. J Bus Econ Stat 10:321–335
Hansen BE (1997) Approximate asymptotic p values for structural-change tests. J Bus Econ Stat 15:60–67
Harvey AC (1987) Applications of the Kalman filter in econometrics. In: Bewley T (ed) Advances in econometrics. I. Cambridge University Press, Fifth World Congress, Vol, pp 285–313
Harvey A (1997) Trends, cycles and autoregressions. Econ J 107:192–201
Hendry DF, Juselius K (2000) Explaining cointegration analysis: part 1. Energy J 21:1–42
Hendry DF, Juselius K (2001) Explaining cointegration analysis: part II. Energy J 22:75–120
Holtedahl P, Joutz FL (2004) Residential electricity demand in Taiwan. Energy Econ 26:201–224
Hunt LC, Salgado C, Thorpe A (1999) The policy of power and the power of policy: energy policy in Honduras. J Energy Dev 25:1–36
Hunt LC, Judge G, Ninomiya Y (2003) Underlying trends and seasonality in UK energy demand: a sectoral analysis. Energy Econ 25:93–118
Ibrahim IB, Hurst C (1990) Estimating energy and oil demand functions: a study of thirteen developing countries. Energy Econ 12:93–102
Inglesi R (2010) Aggregate electricity demand in South Africa: conditional forecasts to 2030. Appl Energy 87:197–204
Inglesi-Lotz R (2011) The evolution of price elasticity of electricity demand in South Africa: a Kalman filter application. Energy Policy 39:3690–3696
Johansen S (1991) Estimation and hypothesis testing of cointegration vectors in Gaussian vector autoregressive models. Econom 59:1551–1580
Jumbe CB (2004) Cointegration and causality between electricity consumption and GDP: empirical evidence from Malawi. Energy Econ 26:61–68
Kalman RE (1960) A new approach to linear filtering and prediction problems. J Basic Eng 82:35–45
Kalman RE (1963) New methods in Wiener filtering theory. In: Bogdanoff JL, Kozin F (eds) Proceeding of the first symposium on engineering applications of random function theory and probability. John Wiley and Sons, New York, pp 270–388
Keho Y (2016) What drives energy consumption in developing countries? The experience of selected African countries. Energy Policy 91:233–246
Kiviet JF (1995) On bias, inconsistency, and efficiency of various estimators in dynamic panel data models. J Econom 68:53–78
Lawson T (1980) Adaptive expectations and uncertainty. Rev Econ Stud 47:305–320
Masreliez C, Martin R (1977) Robust Bayesian estimation for the linear model and robustifying the Kalman filter. IEEE Trans Automat Contr 22:361–371
Milani F (2007) Expectations, learning and macroeconomic persistence. J Monet Econ 54:2065–2082
Ministry of New and Renewable Energy (2012) Guidelines for tariff based competitive bidding process for grid connected power projects based on renewable energy sources. Ministry of New and Renewable Energy, Government of India
Ministry of New and Renewable Energy (2015) Green energy corridor project. Press Information Bureau, Government of India
Morisson GW, Pike DH (1977) Kalman filter applied to statistical forecasting. Manag Sci 23:768–774
Nakajima T, Hamori S (2010) Change in consumer sensitivity to electricity prices in response to retail deregulation: a panel empirical analysis of the residential demand for electricity in the United States. Energy Policy 38:2470–2476
Phillips PCB, Perron P (1988) Testing for a unit root in time series regression. Biom 75:335–346
Pouris A (1987) The price elasticity of electricity demand in South Africa. Appl Econ 19:1269–1277

Sbia R, Shahbaz M, Hamdi H (2014) A contribution of foreign direct investment, clean energy, trade openness, carbon emissions and economic growth to energy demand in UAE. Econ Model 36:191–197

Shahbaz M, Tang CF, Shabbir MS (2011) Electricity consumption and economic growth nexus in Portugal using cointegration and causality approaches. Energy Policy 39:3529–3536

Sinha A, Bhattacharya J (2014) Is economic liberalization causing environmental degradation in India? An analysis of interventions. J Appl Bus Econ 16:121–136

Sinha A, Shahbaz M (2018) Estimation of environmental Kuznets curve for CO_2 emission: role of renewable energy generation in India. Renew Energy 119:703–711

Slade ME (1989) Modelling stochastic and cyclical components of technical change: an application of the Kalman filter. J Econom 41:363–383

TERI (2017) Transitions in Indian electricity sector: 2017–2030. The Energy and Resources Institute

Thamae RI, Thamae LZ, Thamae TM (2015) Dynamics of electricity demand in Lesotho: A Kalman filter approach. Stud Bus Econ 10:130–139

United Nations (2015) Sustainable development goals. Department of Public Information, United Nations

Wiener N (1949) Extrapolation, interpolation and smoothing of stationary time series with engineering applications. MIT Press, Cambridge, MA

World Bank (2016) World bank indicators. Retrieved from http://data.worldbank.org/indicator

Zaman K, Khan MM, Ahmad M, Rustam R (2012) Determinants of electricity consumption function in Pakistan: old wine in a new bottle. Energy Policy 50:623–634

Zivot E, Andrews D (1992) Further evidence of the great crash, the oil-price shock, and the unit-root hypothesis. J Bus Econ Stat 10:251–270

Sahbi Farhani holds a M.Sc. in Statistics Applied to Management from the Higher Institute of Management of Sousse (ISG Sousse), University of Sousse, TUNISIA (2009) and a Ph.D. in Economic Sciences from the Faculty of Economic Sciences and Management of Tunis (FSEGT), University of Tunis El Manar, Tunisia (2017).

In September 2020, he was appointed as an Assistant Professor of Quantitative Methods at the Higher Institute of Finance and Taxation of Sousse (Institut Supérieur de Finances et de Fiscalité de Sousse, ISFFS), University of Sousse, Tunisia.

Between April 2019 and September 2020, he joined the post of Director at the Private Faculty of Management and Sciences of Administration of Sousse (FMSA Sousse), Tunisia. Between August 2017 and July 2018, he joined the Private High School of Economics and Management of Sousse, the Private University of Sousse, Tunisia as a General Director. Previously, he served as a Director of Studies and Internships at the same university (September 2016-August 2017). He also served the position of Assistant professor of Quantitative Methods and Head of Department (October 2014- August 2018) at The Private University of Sousse, and Research-assistant of Quantitative Methods at the Faculty of Pharmacy of Monastir, University of Monastir, Tunisia (October 2010-September 2015). Dr. Sahbi FARHANI is also a Non-Resident Researcher at the IPAG Business School, Paris, France (since January 2014), and a Visiting researcher at the University of Lille 3, France (since March 2015). Dr. Sahbi FARHANI is a researcher in Energy Economics and Econometrics. His research areas concern energy economics, environmental degree of pollution, and climate change. His articles are published in refereed journals such as Energy Policy, Energy, Renewable and Sustainable Energy Reviews, Journal of Energy and Development, International Journal of Energy Sector Management, Environmental Science and Pollution Research, Economic Modelling, Structural Change and Economic Dynamics, etc.

Smart Grids as a Step Toward Global Warming Objective: A Comparative Analysis Between the United States, China and Japan

Khouloud Senda Bennani

Abstract This study aims for a better understanding of the link between CO_2 emissions, global warming and the development of Smart Grids (SGs). This was based on a comparison between the United States, China and Japan. These three countries are classified as the main polluters of the planet, characterized as being very vulnerable to global warming and known as global leaders in the development of the SGs.

Keywords Global warming · Smart grids · United states · China · Japan

1 Introduction

Today, more than half of the world's population lives in urban areas. This urban concentration continues to grow in line with population growth. Thus, cities concentrate the majority of greenhouse gas (CO_2) emissions from the residential, tertiary, industrial and transportation sectors. With this human carbon footprint, cities become highly vulnerable to extreme climate change (droughts, floods, storms) (Edenhifer et al. 2014; Jackson et al. 2018; Jevrejeva et al. 2018; Pichler et al. 2017). Due to the very long lifetime of CO_2 in the atmosphere, the global average temperature has increased by about 1 °C compared to pre-industrial levels (Peters et al. 2012; IPCC 2018; He et al. 2020). This temperature could increase by 2 °C to 5 °C by 2100 (IPCC 2018, 2019). In particular, environmental issues have become increasingly important in the energy sector. Several new issues related to climate change, the scarcity of energy resources, the resulting increase in energy prices, and impacts on the environment and human health are already beginning to emerge (IPCC 2018; Pichler et al. 2017). To meet these challenges, the energy transition has become necessary. This consists in the transition from the current energy model, characterized by a high level of consumption and production mainly based on fossil resources that emit CO_2 and are responsible for climate change, to a less centralized system based on distributed and renewable sources using modern and intelligent technologies that are less energy

K. S. Bennani (✉)
UTC, Carthage, Tunisia
e-mail: senda.bennani@utctunisie.com

S. Goutte et al. (eds.), *Advances in Managing Energy and Climate Risks*,
Lecture Notes in Energy 82, https://doi.org/10.1007/978-3-030-71403-1_5

consuming. This energy transition concerns all uses of energy: thermal energy, heat, fuels used for mobility and electricity.

More specifically, this study aims to clarify the link between climate change and the electric power sector. It also presents the genesis of Smart Girls (SGs) as tools to guide energy policy decisions in order to address environmental and energy issues. This study presents a comparative analysis between the United States, China and Japan, the main contributors to global warming in the world (Worldatlas 2019). The combined share of global CO_2 transfers by China and the United States was higher than that of any other country or region, with more than a third of the total for all years (Davis et al. 2011; Li et al. 2020). Japan is the world's 5th largest CO_2 emitting country and its inhabitants live in high-risk areas, vulnerable to various natural hazards (Sundermann et al. 2013). These three countries have committed to international climate goals including the recent Paris Agreement objectives. They have all opted for SGs to meet these objectives. However, these networks have had different trajectories given the contextual specificities of each country.

2 Emergence of the Smart Grids Concept

The means of extraction developed by certain countries and their use of unconventional resources (gas from source rock, oil sands and shales) to cope with the depletion of fossil resources, have not met with major success in terms of social acceptability (Bouckaert 2013). These alternative means can lead to pollution of the surrounding water tables or rivers by the chemical contents used in the processes and the waste they produce. There are even countries such as France and Germany that have banned the extraction of oil shale because of its environmental effects (Bouckaert 2013). In response to the devastating climate disasters threatening the globe, 196 countries and entities signed a historic climate text in Paris (UNFCCC 2015). This agreement aims to limit global warming to well below 2 °C by reducing CO_2 emissions.

In addition, with the climate challenges that are already taking shape around the world, access to networks and basic services, such as water and energy, will deteriorate. Let's take the example of electrical energy, with millions of homes producing and storing this resource, the electrical distribution network is becoming more complex and extremely expensive in terms of electricity and money. Hence the need and the urgency to adopt new functionalities in order optimize the distribution and consumption of electricity energy with minimum emissions (Liu et al. 2020; Wang et al. 2018). As a result, many countries around the world have changed their energy policies and turned to alternative energies such as Smart Grids. The electricity sector is one of the most polluting sectors and one of those where improvements appear to be most accessible (Bouckaert 2013). Successfully switching to SGs can significantly reduce emissions in a cost-effective manner (EDF 2017; IEA 2017). They contribute to climate change mitigation by allowing more renewable electricity to be included in the grid and by promoting the efficiency, reliability and flexibility of the power system (EPRI 2008; Stephens et al. 2013). They also contribute to climate change adaptation by increasing the resilience of power systems to severe and disruptive weather events such as Storm Sandy and malicious attacks on the grid (Feldpausch-Parker et al. 2018; Koenigs et al. 2013; Morgan et al. 2009; Stephens et al. 2008).

3 Smart Grid: What Is It?

Smart Grids contain a variety of interconnected technologies, including smart meters, advanced sensors and other technology configurations. By relying on these technologies, it becomes possible to make the traditional electrical infrastructure "talk" and retrieve valuable data. They enable consumers to closely monitor the amount of energy they consume and suppliers to regulate the distribution of power according to the needs of households and other consumers (businesses, communities, etc.). Unlike traditional power grids, which are characterized by controlled electricity production and uncontrolled consumption, SGs involve all producers, distributors and consumers of electrical energy in the management of the network (Table 1).

Table 1 Differences between traditional Grids and Smart Grids

Traditional grids	Smart grids
– Supply follows demand – One-way communication with no feedback from the electricity consumer side – Top-down model where electricity is generated in bulk centralized units – Centralized generation – Not possible for the consumer to monitor his hourly electricity consumption – Limited sensors – All problems can only be solved manually – High rate of system interruptions and blackouts – Limited control – Limited choice to customers – Meter reading supply only limited information about the grid condition – Slow response time – Contribute to carbon emissions	– Demand follows supply – Two-way communication between the utility and the electricity consumer – Distributed generation – Sensors throughout – Self-monitoring and self-healing process – Possibility of reducing the electricity bill by controlling consumption – There's an option for adaptive islanding – Pervasive control – Multiple choice to customers – Smart meters allow utilities to collect the required information frequently – Reliable, secure and dependable electrical service – Provide real-time information of all the events (consumption, errors, defaults, etc.) – Reduction of carbon emissions

Source Al Khuffash (2018), Berst (2011), Gao et al. (2012), Majeed Butt et al. (2020)

4 Energy Transition in the United States

The United States is the world's leading economic power. It is energy secure and independent since it is the main producer of non-conventional resources. Their level of independence could reach 97% in 2035 (IEA 2012 and 2013). They are among the main polluters of the planet (EPA 2020). In order to combat climate change and adapt to its consequences, President Barack Obama has lobbied for the United States to sign the Paris agreement (Tapia Granados and Spash 2019). However, in 2017, Donald Trump's U.S. federal government announced that it would no longer participate in the global climate change mitigation efforts provided for in the charters of this agreement. In the face of opposition and climate denial from the Trump's federal government, "We Are Still In" and "American's Pledge" were launched in 2017 to ensure that the United States remains a global leader in reducing CO_2 emissions and meets the country's ambitious climate targets under the Paris agreement. Indeed, since the launch of these organizations, climate action by non-federal US leaders has increased dramatically (America's Pledge & We Are Still In 2020).

The United States' first steps towards Smart Grids technology began in 2003 with the publication of the "Grid 2030" report in which the State announced its national vision for the second 100 years of electricity. In 2007, the United States enacted the Energy Independence and Security Act (EISA) in which it codified the policy for implementing a comprehensive smart grid in the country. This federal policy provides funding of $100 million per year for five years starting in 2008 for the development and enhancement of SGs capabilities (Majeed Butt et al. 2020). In 2009, a new law was passed, the American Recovery and Reinvestment Act, which provided $11.4 billion to accelerate the development and deployment of SGs (Majeed Butt et al. 2020; Muto 2017). Investments in SGs deployment have demonstrated SGs projects and 22 related services in five different states (Majeed Butt et al. 2020). U.S. SGs projects are segmented according to the following elements: Advanced Metering Infrastructure, Customer Systems, Electric Distribution Systems, Electric Transmission Systems, Equipment Manufacturing, Integrated and/or Crosscutting Systems. The arrival in 2009 of a non-governmental entity, the North American Energy Standards Board (NAESB), to support the accelerated deployment of SGs (Mutto 2017), has enabled faster development of interoperability standards (Eisen 2013). The pace of progress of SGs projects was variable because it depended largely on decisions made at the utility, state and local levels (Campbell 2018; DOE 2014). Between 2010 and 2015, $8 billion of investment has been made for SGs deployment. More than 50% of the investment has been made in Advanced Metering Infrastructure (AMI). The United States ranked 2nd behind China as the world's largest investor in renewable energy, excluding hydropower. By 2016, the U.S. power grid is comprised of more than 7300 power plants, nearly 160,000 miles of high-voltage power lines and millions of miles of low-voltage power lines and distribution transformers, connecting 145 million customers nationwide (EIA 2016). In 2017, 39 U.S. states have taken a total of 288 policy and deployment actions related to power grid modernization, tariff reform, and the implementation of advanced metering infrastructure and microgrids (US. Department of energy 2018).

5 Energy Transition in China

China is a developing country, highly populated and highly industrialized (Chaponnière and Lautier 2014; Lin and Zhu 2017; Wang and Ma 2018). It is a country that was the world's tenth economic power in 1980, and since has become the second largest country in the world in terms of GDP behind the United States. This evolution was possible due to an enormous production of energy (Maréchal 2013). Moreover, China is considered to be the world's largest emitter and user of coal-fired energy (Ngar-yin Mah 2019; He et al. 2020). China's economic growth has resulted in massive CO_2 emissions (Wang et al. 2015; Zhang and Zhao 2019). In 30 years these emissions have jumped from 1.4 to 7.2 Gt (Maréchal 2013). As a result, the country faces enormous pressure to reduce CO_2 emissions to avoid the catastrophic consequences of climate change (Yang et al. 2019). Some believe that it will be very difficult to achieve the objective of controlling global warming if the pace of China's CO_2 emissions does not slow down (Cohen et al. 2019). Thus, China has set significant targets for reducing its carbon emissions and energy consumption (METI 2017; NDRC 2016; Zhang 2017; Yang et al. 2019). Indeed, China promised by signing the COP21 climate agreement in Paris in 2016 that the relative share of coal in China's energy mix will increase from 65% in 2016 to 55% in 2020 and that of green energy from 12 to 15%. To achieve this, China is counting on Smart Grids.

Since the 2000s, the country has focused on the construction of ultra-high voltage SGs (Mah et al. 2017; Zpryme 2011). The two monopolistic state-owned grid companies, the State Grid Corporation of China (SGCC) and the China Southern Power Grid (CSG), have launched major SG plans. The years 2009 and 2010 were devoted to planning and technical testing, before the bulk of the grid is deployed between 2011 and 2015. From 2016 to 2020, the grid is being upgraded to achieve full deployment by 2020. Currently, China's smart grid has made great strides in terms of philosophy, technology, equipment and engineering practices (Xiao et al. 2020). China may soon become the largest market in the EES arena, just as it has become the largest T&D market in the world (Xu et al. 2010). This estimate is based on the fact that China has already become the original equipment manufacturer for smart meters offered by the world's major utilities. This makes it possible for this country to build their infrastructure faster and cheaper than anywhere else because of its competitive cost (Xu et al. 2010). Also, China's centralized political leadership and its ability to standardize and replicate play an important role in accelerating the realization of SGs (Xu et al. 2010).

6 Energy Transition in Japan

Japan is a large, wealthy, high-tech industrialized country that is highly dependent on hydrocarbon imports, which in 2010 accounted for more than 60% of its energy mix. As such, it is a country that is particularly vulnerable to the devastating effects of global warming (Sundermann et al. 2013). It regularly suffers from numerous natural disasters due to its geographical position in Asia and the Pacific Rim. The most frequent are typhoons, earthquakes and heat waves. More rarely, tsunamis also occur, usually as a result of earthquakes and volcanic eruptions. This is why Japan had to look for local solutions to its energy situation very early on while trying to respect the environment. Japan's energy needs also soared following the Fukushima disaster in 2011. Indeed, before the Fukushima accident, nuclear power constituted about 30% of the energy mix and was expected to increase to 50% by 2030 (DeWit et al. 2012). Nuclear power was seen as the key to Japan's energy independence and low-carbon future. With the accident, 54 nuclear reactors were shut down and the country turned to thermal power generation using imported natural gas. However, this only increased CO_2 emissions very significantly. Since this accident, the energy and environmental strategy has been revisited many times in the medium and long term (The Denki Shimbum 2013; Mah et al. 2013). Given its vulnerability to the devastating effects of global warming, however, Japan has made a formal commitment to reduce its CO_2 emissions by 2020. Emphasis has been placed on renewable energy production and energy efficiency (Energy and Environment Council 2011). Four large-scale intelligent community demonstration projects were launched in 2010 in four cities, namely Kyoto, Yokohama, Kitakyushu and Toyota (Ngar-yin Mah 2019; Dewit 2014; Mah et al. 2013; Pham 2014). These projects aim to test different technologies and solutions, including photovoltaic production, connected electric vehicles, real-time management of energy flows, etc. The projects are designed to test different technologies and solutions, including photovoltaic production, connected electric vehicles, real-time management of energy flows, etc. The projects will be carried out in the following areas These projects have been financed and led mainly by the Japanese national government and have been supported by Japanese electronics companies (Toshiba, Panasonic, Hitachi, Sharp), but also by other actors such as real estate firms (Languillon-Aussel 2015). In these community projects, the end consumer was at the center of energy use by providing and enabling him to appropriate the technical tools to manage his consumption on his own. The aim of these projects was to promote behavioural changes by adapting to the daily reality of citizens and to identify good practices to be generalised (Ling et al. 2012; Mah et al. 2013). Since the launch of these projects, Japan has seen its energy-related CO_2 emissions decrease at a rapid rate (Table 2).

Table 2 An overview of United States, China and Japan and features of their SGs development

Features	United States	China	Japan
GDP (1961–2018)	– The annual average is 3.05 – The change between 1961 and 2018 is 27%[a] – The highest value (7.24) is recorded in 1984 – The lowest value (−2.54) is recorded in 2009 – In 1961, the relative world share was 53.48% – In 2018, this same share is 95.71%	– The annual average is 8.19 – The change between 1961 and 2018 is 124% – The highest value (19.3) is recorded in 1970 – The lowest value (−27.27) was recorded in 1961 – In 1961, the relative share of this country was -634.14% – In 2018, this same share is 214.72%	– The annual average is 3.67 – The change between 1961 and 2018 is 93% – The highest value (12.88) is recorded in 1968 – The lowest value (−5.42) is recorded in 2009 In 1961 the relative share was 280.06% – In 2018, this same share is 25.78%
Industry	– An industrialized country largely focused on the tertiary sector and relying on innovation	– Rapidly industrialising	– High-tech industrialised
Urban population	– 18% increase in 58 years (1961–2018) – The annual average of 76.27 – The value is expected to hover around 83.59 in 2025	– 265% increase in 58 years (1961–2018) – The annual average is 30.3 – The value is expected to hover around 67.78 in 2025	– 45% increase in 58 years (1961–2018) – The annual average of 78.58 – The value is expected to hover around 92.16 in 2025
Energy sector (in 2019)	– 1st in the world for the production of oil, natural gas, petroleum products, nuclear, geothermal and biomass-based electricity – 2nd in the world for total electricity generation (wind and solar photovoltaic) – 3rd in the world for coal production	– 1st producer and consumer of coal – 1st largest importer of oil and natural gas in the world – 1st largest electricity producer in the world – 1st place for the number of nuclear reactors under construction	– Japan lacks natural energy resources and therefore depends on imports to cover its needs – Japan is the world's 3rd largest importer of natural gas and coal and 4th largest importer of oil
CO_2 Emission	2nd world rank	1st world rank	5th in the world
Electricity consumption	Increase of 221% in 54 years (1960–2014)	604% increase in 54 years (1960–2014)	2484% increase in 43 (1971–2014)

(continued)

Table 2 (continued)

Features	United States	China	Japan
SG development	– The United States was a pioneer in the development of smart grids. Major investments are being made to modernize a faulty and often obsolete power grid – The USA. has undertaken 100 SGs projects; – 31 projects consist of deploying advanced counting systems; – 5 projects involve the integration of SGs functions into buildings, equipment and consumer devices; – 13 projects involve the modernization of the distribution network; – 10 projects concern the modernization of the transportation network; – 2 projects dealing with new equipment, hardware and software; – 39 projects consist of the integration of complex solutions of SG functions	– Incumbent-led model – China has invested heavily in a very high voltage electricity transmission network (UHV). Two regionally monopolised grid companies focus on building super-grids with super high voltage and high capacity across China	– Government-led, community-oriented, and business-driven model – Four large-scale smart community demonstration projects in Yokohama City, Toyota City, Kyoto Prefecture and Kitakyushu City (2010–2014)

[a]The percentages are taken from Perspective Monde

7 Conclusion

In recent decades, natural disasters have multiplied as a result of global warming. Climate change and energy have been commonly linked in the discourse of policy leaders and legislators to mitigate these disasters, often with a focus on reducing carbon emissions from energy systems and the need to improve their resilience. Smart grids are perceived as the pathway to a low carbon emission because of a larger contribution of renewable energy sources. These “non-polluting” energies make it possible to produce electricity while respecting the environment. They are capable of sustaining energy demand without betraying the environmental ambitions of the international community (Paris Agreement). Their deployment demonstrates a country's ability to respond to complex environmental issues.

This study paves the way for further studies exploring how different actors in different institutional contexts are responding to the consequences of climate change and the risks associated with evolving energy systems. Also, it would be interesting to conduct studies that allow a better understanding of the complex dynamics between all stakeholders involved in SGs projects and the diversity of energy transition paths between countries using the multi-level perspective (MLP).

References

Al Khuffash K (2018) Smart grids—Overview and background information. Appl Smart Grid Technol 1–10. 10.1016/b978-0-12-803128-5.00001

America's Pledge & We Are Still In (2020). We are still in to deliver on America's pledge: A retrospective. Bloomberg Philanthropies Support LLC and We Are Still In. https://assets.bbhub.io/dotorg/sites/28/2020/09/We-Are-Still-In-to-Deliver-on-Americas-Pledge_.pdf

Berst J (2011) Smart grid 101, Smart grid news. Available from: https://www.smartgrid.gov/files/Smart_grid_101_Everything_you_wanted_to_know_about_grid_mode_201112.pdf

Bouckaert S (2013) Contribution des Smart Grids à la transition énergétique: évaluation dans des scénarios long terme. Ecole Nationale Supérieure des Mines de Paris, Français

Campbell RJ (2018) The smart grid: status and outlook. Congressional Research Service 7-5700 www.crs.gov R45156

Chaponnière JR, Lautier M (2014) La Chine et l'industrialisation au Sud. Les économies émergentes d'Asie 1(69):27–53

Cohen G, Jalles JT, Loungani P, Marto R, Wang G (2019) Decoupling of emissions and GDP: evidence from aggregate and provincial Chinese data. Energy Economics 77:105–118

Davis SJ, Peters GP, Caldeira K (2011) The supply chain of CO_2 emissions. Proc Natl Acad Sci USA 108:18554–18559

DeWit A (2014) Japan's resilient, decarbonizing and democratic smart communities. Asia-Pac J [en ligne]. 15 décembre 2014. 12:50(3)

Dewit A, Tetsunari I, Masaru K (2012) Fukushima and the political economy of power policy in Jpan. In: Kingston J (ed) Natural disaster and nuclear crisis in Japan: Response and recovery after Japan's 3/11. Routledge, New York, pp 156–172

DOE (2014) Smart grid system report, August 2014. https://www.smartgrid.gov/files/2014-Smart-Grid-SystemReport.pdf

Edenhifer O, Pichs-Madruga R, Sokona Y, Minx JC, Farahani E, Kadner S, Seyboth K, Adler A, Baum I, Brunner S, Eickemeler P, Kriemann B, Savolanien J, Schlomer S, Von Stechow C, Zwickel T (2014) Climate change 2014: mitigation of climate change

EDF (2017) Grid modernization: the foundation for climate change progress. environmental defense fund. Grid Modernization: The Foundation for Climate Change Progress, Washington, DC

EIA (2016) U.S. electric system is made up of interconnections and balancing authorities. https://www.eia.gov/todayinenergy/detail.php?id=27152

Eisen JB (2013) Smart regulation and federalism for the smart grid. Hary Environ Law Rev 37:101–156

Energy and Environment Council (2011) The prime minister in action. http://japan.kantei.go.jp/kan/actions/201106/22KAIGI_energy-environment_e.html

EPA (2020) Global greenhouse gas emissions data. https://www.epa.gov/ghgemissions/global-greenhouse-gas-emissions-data

EPRI (2008) The green grid: energy savings and carbon emissions reductions enabled by a Smart Grid-ERPI: Palo Alto, California. http://large.stanford.edu/courses/2015/ph240/xu1/docs/epri-1016905.pdf
Feldpausch-Parker AM, Peterson TR, Stephens JC, Wilson EJ (2018). Smart grid electricity system planning and climate disruptions: a review of climate and energy discourse post-Superstorm Sandy. Renew Sustain Energ Rev 82:1961–1968
Gao J, Xiao Y, Liu J, Liang W, Chen CLP (2012) A survey of communication/networking in Smart Grids. Future Gener Comput Syst 28(2):391–404, 0167–739X. https://doi.org/10.1016/j.future.2011.04.014
He G, Lin J, Zhang Y, Zhang W, Larangeira G, Zhang C, Peng W, Liu M (2020) Perspective enabling a rapid and just transition away from coal in China. One Earth. 3(2):21, 187–194
IEA (2017) Digitialization & energy. International Energy Agency, Paris. http://www.iea.org/publications/freepublications/publication/DigitalizationandEnergy3.pdf
IEA (2012) World energy outlook, 8, 9, 10, 11
IEA (2013) Medium-term oil market report, 8
IPCC (2018) Global warming of 1.5 C. An IPCC special report on the impacts of global warming of 1.5 C above pre-industrial levels and related global greenhouse gas emission pathways, in the context of strengthening the global response to the threat of climate change, sustainable development, and effort to eradicate poverty. https://www.ipcc.ch/site/assets/uploads/sites/2/2019/05/SR15_SPM_version_report_LR.pdf
IPCC (2019) Special report on the ocean and cryosphere in a changing climate. https://www.ipcc.ch/site/assets/uploads/sites/3/2019/12/SROCC_FullReport_FINAL.pdf
Jackson LP, Grinsted A, Jevrejeva S (2018) 21st century sea level rise in line with the Paris accord. Earth's Future 6(2):213–229. https://doi.org/10.1002/2017EF000688
Jevrejeva S, Jackson LP, Grinsted A et al (2018) Flood damage costs under the sea level rise with warming of 1.5 ◦C and 2 °C. Environ Res Lett 13(7):074014. https://doi.org/10.1088/1748-9326/aacc76
Koenigs C, Suri M, Kreiter A, Elling C, Eagles J, Peterson T, Stephens J, Wilson E (2013) A smarter grid for renewable energy: different states of action. Challenges 4(2):217–233
Languillon-Aussel R (2015) Kashiwa no Ha: laboratoire urbain pour les nouveaux enjeux des populations matures. Urbia, n 18
Ling APA, Kokichi S, Masao M (2012) The Japanese smart grid: initiatives, investments and collaborration. Inter J Adv Comput Sci Appl 3(7):1–11
Li Y, Xu D, Wang J, Zhang Y, Yu X (2020) Industrial path analysis for CO_2 transfers induced by final consumption: a comparison of the United States and China. J Clean Prod 251:119604. https://doi.org/10.1016/j.jclepro.2019.119604
Lin B, Zhu J (2017) Energy and carbon intensity in China during the urbanization and industrialization process: A panel VAR approach. J Cleaner Prod 168:780–790
Liu Y, Yu Y, Gao N, Wu F (2020) A grid as smart as the internet. Engineering 6:778–788
Mah DN, Wu Y-Y, Ip JC, Hills PR (2013) The role of the state in sustainable energy transitions: a case study of large smart grid demonstration projects in Japan. Energy Policy 63:726–737. https://doi.org/10.1016/j.enpol.2013.07.106
Mah DN-Y, Wu Y-Y, Hills PR (2017) Explaining the role of incumbent utilities in sustainable energy transitions: a case study of the Smart Grid development in China. Energ Policy 109:794–804
Majeed Butt O, Muhammad Zulqarnain M, Majeed Butt T (2020) Recent advancement in smart grid technology: future prospects in the electrical power network. Ain Shams Eng J
Maréchal J-P (2013) La Chine et le changement climatique. Hérodote 150(3):46
METI (2017) Major stream of energy shifts (The 21st Meeting, Strategic Policy Committee (an advisory committee), Agency for Natural Resources an Energy). Ministry of Economy, Trade and Industry. http://www.enecho.meti.go.jp/en/committe/council/basic_policy_subcommittee/pdf/data170901.pdf

Morgan MG, Apt J, Lave L, Ilic M, Sirbu M, Peha J (2009) The many meanings of Smart Grid, in a briefing note from the department of engineering and public policy, Carnegie Mellon University. Pittsburgh, PA, p 5

Muto S (2017) From laissez-faire to intervention: analysing policy narratives on interoperability standards for the smart grid in the United States. Energy Res Soc Sci 31:111–119

NDRC (2016) The 13 five year plan for economic and social development of the people's republic of China (2016–2020). National Development and Reform commission, Beijing

Ngar-yin Mah D (2019) Conceptualising government-market dynamics in socio-technical energy transitions: a comparative case study of smart grid developments in China and Japan. Geoforum. https://doi.org/10.1016/j.geoforum.2019.07.025

Peters GP, Andrew RM, Boden T, Canadell JG, Ciais P, Le Quéré C, Marland G, Raupach MR, Wilson C (2012) The challenge to keep global warming below 2 °C. Nat Clim Change 3(1):2–4

Pham C (2014) Smart cities in Japan. An assessment on the potential for EU-Japan cooperation and business development. EU-Japan Centre Ind Cooperation (p 67)

Pichler P, Zwickel T, Chavez A, Kretschmer T, Weisz H (2017) Reducing urban greenhouse gas footprints. Scu Rep 7:14659

Schrottke J et al (2019) Adaptation is job one: business need to prepare for the impacts of extreme weather and disruptive climate change. Futurist 47:6

Stephens J, Wilson E, Peterson T, Meadowcroft J (2013) Getting smart? Climate change and the electric grid. Challenges 4(2):201–216

Sundermann L, Schelske O, Hausmann P (2013) Mind the risk. A global ranking of cities under threat from natural disasters. SwissRE, Zuirch

Tapia Granadosa JA, Spash CL (2019) Policies to reduce CO_2 emissions: fallacies and evidence from the United. States and California. Environ Sci Policy 94:262–266

The Denki Shimbum (2013) Prime minister Abe directs review of energy and environmental strategy. The Denki Shimbun, 29 January

UNFCCC (2015) Paris Agreement, United Nations. https://unfccc.int/sites/default/files/english_paris_agreement.pdf

US. Department of energy (2018) Smart grid system report to congress, United States Department of Energy Washington, DC 20585

Wang S, Ma Y (2018) Influencing factors and regional discrepancies of the efficiency of carbon dioxide emissions in Jiangsu, China. Ecol Ind 90:460–468

Wang Q, Chiu YH, Chiu CR (2015) Driving factors behind carbon dioxide emissions in China: Aamodified production-theoretical decomposition analysis. Energ Economics 51:252–260

Wang Y, Qiu H, Tu Y, Liu Q, Ding Y, Wang W (2018) A review of smart metering for future Chinese grids. Energy Procedia 152:1194–1199

Worldatlas (2019) https://www.worldatlas.com/articles/biggest-contributors-to-global-warming-in-the-world.html

Xu D, Wang M, Wu C, Chan K (2010) Evolution of the smart grid in China. Mckinsey & Company, 18–23

Yang J, Cai W, Ma M, Li L, Liu C, Ma X, Li L, Chun X (2019) Driving forces of China's CO_2 emissions from energy consumption based on Kaya-LMDI methods, sciences of the Total Environment 711:134569

Zhang Z (2017) Are China's climate commitments in a post-Paris agreement sufficiently ambitious? Clim change 8(2)

Zhang S, Zhao T (2019) Identifying major influencing factors of CO_2 emissions in China: regional disparities analysis based on STIRPAT Model from 1996 to 2015. Atmos Environ 207:136–147

Zpryme (2011) China: rise of the smart grid (Special report by Zpryme's smart grid insights). Austin, Texas: Zpryme research & consulting

Khouloud Senda Bennani is an Assistant Professor of Management and Head of Lectures at Tunis Carthage University (UTC). She holds a Ph.D. in management sciences from the Higher Institute of Management of Tunis (ISGT) and the National School of Public Administration of Montreal (ENAP). She is a member of the laboratory of Interdisciplinary Research on Changes in Economies and Enterprises (LARIME). She is a reviewer for several international scientific meetings. Her areas of expertise and teaching focus on public management, strategy, entrepreneurship and human resources management. Her scientific research interests are environmental policies and the transformation of national systems of governance and state organizations.

Towards a Better Understanding of the Factors Explaining the Behavior of Green Energy Adoption

Sihem Ben Saad

Abstract The development of green energy is a major concern of our time. This area is undergoing a resurgence of interest, due to rising energy prices and the urgent need to find new sources of energy. The objective of this chapter is to examine the determinants that can contribute to the adoption of green energy including economic factors (Perceived Transparency of Business Practices, Willingness to Pay More), social psychological factors (Perceived Value, Social Influence and Contagion), factors related to national culture (Personality Traits, Demographic Aspects), factors related to the environment (Environmental Knowledge, Environmental Awareness). These determinants would help formulate strategies that encourage consumers to voluntarily adopt green energy. This chapter shows that government regulations are not sufficient to adopt green energy. Indeed, consumers are also motivated by emotional, social, cultural, environmental and economic considerations. Likewise, policy makers could formulate mass messages that make consumers feel responsible and develop a green orientation.

Keywords Green energy · Green energy consumption · Perceived value · Lifestyle · Personality traits · Willingness to pay more

1 Introduction

Conducting research in sustainable development has become a major concern for researchers and governments (Shove et al. 2015; Upham et al. 2015). Sustainable development can help alleviate the problems associated with the growing scarcity of energy resources and the adverse effects of climate change. However, environmental sustainability can never be achieved without clean energy sources (i.e. renewable energy sources or what is also called green energy). Green energy is clean energy whose exploitation produces only negligible quantities of pollutants compared to other more widespread sources (e.g., petroleum products, gas). Different sources of green energy exist. Geothermal power, wind power and solar power are the main

S. Ben Saad (✉)
Carthage Business School, University of Tunis Carthage, Tunisia, Tunisia

S. Goutte et al. (eds.), *Advances in Managing Energy and Climate Risks*,
Lecture Notes in Energy 82, https://doi.org/10.1007/978-3-030-71403-1_6

ones. Due to its ability to reduce environmental damage, green energy has attracted the interest of a growing number of studies (Kondoh 2009; Sarzynski et al. 2012; Shove et al. 2015; Upham et al. 2015; Chandel et al. 2016; Bozorg et al. 2017).

Because several countries are considered to be the largest consumers of energy in the world and emit the most CO_2, the transition to green energy is essential for achieving environmental goals (Sarzynski et al. 2012; Upham et al. 2015). Kostakis and Sardianou (2012) argued that the use of green energy is considered a relevant solution to climate change. It can be used to fight against global warming (Herbes and Ramme 2014). For instance, as the world's largest energy consumer, China is facing pressure amid environmental impacts, including global warming and air pollution. To this end, China is moving towards sustainable development (Xingang et al. 2012; Upham et al. 2015; Hao et al. 2015; Bozorg et al. 2017). Liu et al. (2013) examined the rural social acceptance of renewable energy deployment in eastern China. Liu et al. showed that rural residents are generally favorable to the development of renewable energies.

In addition, the authors presented that carbon emissions had increased fivefold between 1985 and 2006 in the city of Shanghai and that, it is now ranked among the most CO_2 emitting cities in China (Chen et al. 2015).

Several researchers showed support for the idea that countries must reduce greenhouse gas emissions (Chandel et al. 2016; Kondoh 2009; Sarzynski et al. 2012). The widely shared view is that renewable energy or green energy is the relevant solution to tackle the greenhouse gas emission problem. For example, Iceland is the first country in the world in terms of energy produced per capita, with 100% of the energy consumed in the country being green and renewable. In France, the share of renewable energies has increased from 6.6% in 2007 to 10.7% in 2017. Renewable energies in France are the fourth primary energy source in 2017, behind nuclear (40.0%), petroleum products (28.9%) and gas (15.7%). Beyond this trend, the primary consumption of renewable energy fluctuates from year to year. The significant use of primary production of renewable energies since 2005 is mainly due to the development of biofuels, heat pumps and wind power. However, unlike most of developed countries, consumption of green energy is considered limited in developing economies.

Several factors may explain the adoption of green energy. Some studies have shown that government regulations are not enough to induce the adoption of green energy (Xingang et al. 2012; Upham et al. 2015; Hao et al. 2015). Indeed, the will to embrace green energy and the contribution to the well-being of the environment should primarily come from consumers. Reducing energy consumption, improving energy efficiency and increasing the consumption of green energy sources are the main visions for achieving environmental goals. In addition to global and regional renewable energy policies, it is important to sensibilize people about the use of green energy and its positive impacts on sustainable development.

The objective of this chapter is to study the factors that encourage consumers to adopt green energy. The literature review carried out suggests several factors and in particular psychological social factors, factors related to culture, factors related to environment as well as economic factors.

The reminder of the chapter is organized as follows. We start defining green energy. Second, we introduce the concept of green consumer behavior. Third, we discuss the explanatory factors behind the adoption of green energy. Fourth, we examine the social psychological factors. Fifith, we develop the factors related to culture and the factors related to environment. Finally, we present the economic factors that may also explain the adoption of green energy.

2 What Is Green Energy?

Green energy has attracted the attention of several researchers (Zarnikau 2003; Shrimali and Kniefel 2011; Kostakis and Sardianou 2012; Herbes and Ramme 2014). According to Zarnikau (2003), green energy refers to electricity that involves technologies such as biomass projects, solar photovoltaic panels, wind farms and geothermal projects. Thus green energy is generated through renewable energy sources. Kostakis and Sardianou (2012) argued that green energy can be used to deal with global warming. It does not involve any greenhouse gas emissions. The use of green energy sources offers a sustainable solution to climate change.

Most governments around the world have focused on generating electricity using renewable energy sources (Shrimali and Kniefel 2011; Herbes and Ramme 2014). In fact, numerous countries are launching incentive programs to encourage private investment such as feed-in tariffs, captive production and privileged access to networks for renewable energy producers. We can cite the case of the Dutch government which liberalized the green electricity market.

To stimulate demand for green energy in the residential customer segment, the Dutch government has offered relatively generous tax incentives. Shrimali et al. (2013) provide another example of the Indian government. To encourage renewable energy, India has launched several incentive programs, such as renewable energy certificates, accelerated depreciation benefits. Due to the liberalization of the electricity market, consumers in many Indian cities (Mumbai, Ahmedabad, Surat, New Delhi, Bangalore, etc.), can choose from which supplier, they buy the electricity while ensuring that the energy was produced from renewable sources.

3 What Is Green Consumer Behavior?

With the deterioration of the environmental system, consumers are looking for products that preserve their health. This requires specific consumer behavior. This behavior is renamed sustainable behavior or said to be green.

In recent decades, sustainable or green consumer behavior has gained momentum and evolved with changes in business offerings. Fisk (1974) introduced the notion of green consumer behavior in his theory of responsible consumption.

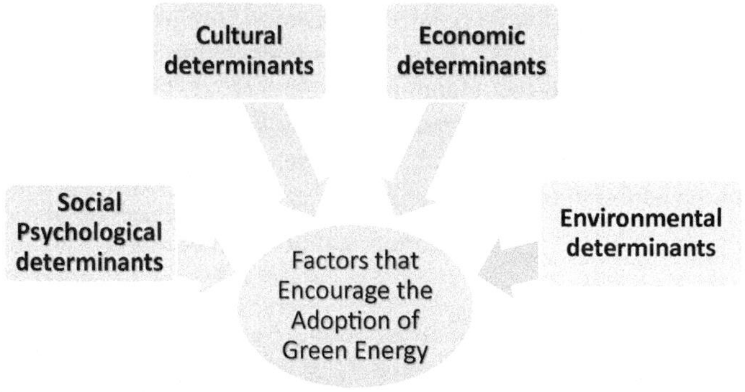

Fig. 1 Factors that encourage the adoption of green energy

According to Lebel and Lorek (2008), green consumer behavior refers to any act that commits the consumer to adopt a given product with the objective of respecting health and the environment. This behavior involves improving oneself wisely for the good of all. Green consumer behavior is the set of physical and mental reactions that a consumer expresses towards sustainable products. In the 1990s, the work of Ellen et al. (1991) and Grunet (1993) restricted green consumption behavior to energy saving and recycling. This notion has broadened to new concepts such as attitude, buying, and motivation (Soonthonsmai 2001). Several studies added the idea that embarking on green or ethical consumer behavior is not an obvious vision (Akbar et al. 2014).

In terms of consumer behavior towards green energy, a limited amount of research lends itself to revealing the factors influencing the adoption decision. The decision to adopt green energy is conditioned by instantaneous determinants.

Social psychological determinants, cultural determinants, environmental determinants and economic determinants are paramount variables in explaining the adoption of green energy. Figure 1 below illustrates the determinants that encourage the adoption of green energy.

4 The Social Psychological Determinants of the Adoption of Green Energy

To explain the adoption behavior of green energy, several studies have addressed factors of a social nature, such as perceived value and social influence.

4.1 Perceived Value

The value perceived by the consumer is one of the variables that contributes to the development of the consumption of green energy. To improve consumer perception of benefits, Hartmann and Apaolaza-Ibanez (2012) argued that the success of green energy adoption depends on the effectiveness of the marketing strategies designed. Indeed, the adoption of green energy by the consumer would depend on the value he perceives.

Recently, energy researchers add the idea that the value perceived by the consumer is an explanatory variable of the evaluations of a given product and of future purchasing decisions (Holbrook 1999; Wüstenhagen et al. 2007; Barlow and Maul 2000; Gale 1994; Yang et al. 2015). In determining the attractiveness of a given product, the perceived value by the consumer is a decisive factor (Zeithaml 1988; Lindgreen et al. 2012). In the literature on environmental and green marketing, Sangraya and Nayak (2017) asserted that green perceived value is a multidimensional construct made up of functional, conditional, emotional and social value. This claim was made on the basis of the work of Hartmann and Apoalaza-Ibanez (2012) and Massini and Menichetti (2012) who advanced the idea that a consumer of green energy considers different types of benefits (utilitarian, psychological and social).

Other approaches have been proposed to understand the meaning of the value associated with consumptions and possessions. The approach of Lai (1995) was retained as it has been the subject of empirical application.

4.1.1 Functional Value

According to Sheth et al. (1991), functional value refers to "the perceived utility acquired from the product from an alternative of functional, utility or physical performance" (p. 160). Lai (1995) suggested that functional value corresponds to the utilitarian, physical and practical performance of the product and derives from its tangible and concrete attributes. This value is estimated after a rational analysis on the part of the consumer which consists in weighing the various benefits accompanying the purchase of the product. Indeed, a rational consumer would try to obtain the maximum benefit with the least possible cost. The study by Kaenzig et al. (2013) examined the role of various attributes of green energy in creating value for consumers. They concluded that the environmental attributes of green energy are vital for customers. Another study by Long et al. (2014) on domestic consumers showed that price was the main factor in consumer behavior in terms of energy saving. Another stream of research states that green energy products offer benefits similar to the advantages offered by conventional energy products. They also offer additional functional benefits, such as reductions in electricity bills and reduction in the production of harmful products (Zeithaml 1988; Prakash 2002; Ibanez et al. 2006; Bozorg et al. 2017; Baležentis and Štreimikien 2019).

4.1.2 Social Value

According to Lai (1995), social value relates to the associations of the product with status and social class. The search for social status by consumers when using a particular product has been mentioned in the study by (Zeithaml 1988; Nelissen and Meijers 2011; Baležentis and Štreimikien 2019). The consumer seeks to identify with a specific social status.

The search for a desired social status has a significant impact on the consumer's attitudes, their motivations and their commitment to a specific consumption behavior. Sangroya and Nayak (2017) added the idea that social value involves the individual perception of what others would think or how they would react to a purchase made by someone. Another study by Douglas (2002) asserts that in addition to economic reasons, consumers buy products to create and maintain social relationships. To this end, several studies have confirmed the significant and positive impact of social norms on consumers' decision to use green products (Salazar et al. 2013; Ek and Matti 2014). The studies carried out go in the same direction as the research of Noppers et al. (2014) who believe that consumers are motivated to use green products because of their functional and symbolic attributes. According to Fennis and Pruyn (2007), symbolic attributes refer to assigning a positive image to the consumer when he buys a given product.

Because they allow consumers to signal their statuses and identities, symbolic attributes can encourage the adoption of sustainable products. Other research suggests that societal norms and values have a significant impact on consumers' choice to adopt green products (Zeithaml 1988; Mignon and Bergek 2012; Faiers et al. 2007; Baležentis and Štreimikien 2019).

4.1.3 Emotional or Affective Value

Emotional or affective worth has been cited in several studies that emphasize the importance of taking into account the emotional dimension in assessing perceived worth (Wiedmann et al. 2007). According to Hartmann et al. (2005), the effect of emotions is much greater when a consumer purchases green products. Lai (1995) stipulated that emotional or affective value results from the product's ability to arouse feelings in the consumer. Lai added the idea that emotions are a key factor in the buying process.

Emotional value refers to the perceived utility gained from the product's ability to arouse curiosity (Zeithaml 1988; Sheth et al. 1991). Emotional value refers to the feelings a consumer experiences during an act of purchase. Wüstenhagen and Bilharz (2006) conducted empirical research on green energy consumers. They have found that the feeling of well-being is the only reason for consuming green energy. Other studies have found a significant relationship between the consumption of green energy and emotional benefits (Zeithaml 1988; Holbrook 2006; Hansla 2011; Hansla et al. 2008; Herbes and Ramme 2014; Baležentis and Štreimikien 2019). For these reasons, Hartmann and Apaolaza-Ibáñez (2012) believe that green energy marketing campaigns should focus on psychological benefits such as self-expressing benefits.

4.1.4 The Conditional or Situational Value

Lai (1995) defines conditional value as the ability of the product to satisfy the constraints of the situation and increase other benefits. According to Sheth et al. (1991), the conditional value corresponds to the perceived utility acquired by an alternative as a result of a set of circumstances facing the decision maker. In addition, the situational value of a given product depends on various economic, social, physical or environmental situations that may enhance the functional value of the product. Lorenzoni et al. (2007) added that the idea that several contextual factors create structural and situational environments that can facilitate or restrict pro-environment behaviors. Rebates, grants, incentives and other incentives motivate customers to invest in energy efficiency projects.

Laws, regulations, availability of green products, environmental concerns, rebates, subsidies are examples of situations that could be incentives to develop green energy (Caird et al. 2008; Sovacool and Ratan 2012; Tsoutsos et al. 2009; Haas et al. 1999; Mignon and Bergek 2012; Herbes and Ramme 2014).

These are the main factors that can influence the purchasing behavior of consumers' green products.

Besides perceived value, the social influence of others is a determinant in explaining green consumption behavior.

4.2 Social Influence and Contagion

Because green consumption behavior is a derivative of socially responsible behavior, several studies have shown that social influence is the most important factor in explaining green adoption (Gupta and Ogden 2009). This concept is an important scientific trend in the study of current consumption patterns. Since a consumer is part of a social group (family, friends, etc.), he can follow them and adopt the same green consumption practices. To this end, it can be argued that the influence of others can significantly determine the green orientation. Regarding social contagion, this concept designates a behavioral mode that people of the same social group adopt to imitate a person considered as a "model". This makes this behavior dominant and may even spread to other social groups (Gosling et al. 1996). Other research suggests that the cultural dimension can significantly explain green behavior.

5 The Cultural Determinants of the Adoption of Green Energy

National culture has always guided the experience of consumers, either by following a particular lifestyle, by building personality traits, or by designing demographic characters. In green behavior, research by Haanpaa (2007) stated that lifestyle positively and significantly determines green engagement and consumer choice. Other work shows that sustainable behavior is well guided by lifestyle, which is accompanied by considerable environmental concern (Hanpaa 2007; Gatersleben et al. 2010; Kinnear et al. 1974).

5.1 Personality Traits

Personality traits are considered a predictive determinant in determining consumption choice and consumer behavioral decision (Whitmarsh and O'Neill 2010). Several studies have addressed the importance of personality traits in green ecological behavior (Diamantopoulos et al. 2003; Kinnear et al. 1974). To this end, it can be said that this factor is explanatory of the pro-environmental behavior of individuals.

5.2 Demographic Aspects

In marketing studies, demographic aspects are evident in explaining consumer behavior. The research by Diamantopoulos et al. (2003) studied the impact of several variables, such as age, marital status, sex, social class, etc. on the intention of green behavioral adoption. This study demonstrated the significant and positive impact of certain demographic variables on the pro-environmental behavior of consumers. Some studies show that environmental determinants are essential to explain the intention of consumers to consume green energy. Other research suggests that the environmental dimension can significantly explain green behavior.

6 The Environmental Determinants of the Adoption of Green Energy

To adopt green energy, environmental knowledge, awareness, concern and the search for well-being can significantly determine green orientation.

6.1 Environmental Knowledge

Consumers become vigilant in their behavior when they are aware of what is harmful to the environment. Several studies show that environmental knowledge significantly influences consumers' intention to consume green energy (Hirschman 1980; Kondoh 2009; Sarzynski et al. 2012; Shove et al. 2015; Chandel et al. 2016; Bozorg et al. 2017).

6.2 Environmental Awareness

Some studies advanced the idea that environmentally conscious consumers can have a significant and positive impact on their green behaviors (Shove et al. 2015; Chandel et al. 2016; Bozorg et al. 2017). These show that the more a consumer is informed about environmental issues, the more he is involved in pro-environmental behavior.

Involvement is an "unobservable state that reflects an individual's interest, excitement, or emotional attachment to a given product" (Bloch 1982). The emergence of this concept is attributed to the high personal importance of an act of purchase by the consumer (Zaichkowsky 1985). Ben Miled-Chérif (2001) considers that "the implication is based on the intensity of the relationship between the product, the needs and the values of the individual".

The latter believe that the involvement can be lasting. According to Bloch (1982), sustainable involvement translates into an interest and a personal attachment to the long-term product. In addition, lasting involvement is considered a stable and permanent state of the consumer towards a product or brand (Houston and Rothschild 1978).

6.3 Environmental Concern

Crosby et al. (1981) demonstrate that environmental concern is a significant determinant of pro-environmental decision-making behavior. Environmental concern is an expressive feeling while environmental awareness is a simple predictive analysis.

6.4 The Search for Well-Being

The search for well-being is a considerable determinant in the green orientation. Research advances the idea that consumers have become very concerned about their consumption, which encourages them to seek their well-being (Chandel et al. 2016).

7 The Economic Determinants of the Adoption of Green Energy

To explain the adoption behavior of green energy, some research has focused on the economic aspect. The willingness to pay more (green value/price), the perceived transparency of business practices and individual income are variables that may be significant determinants of the green orientation.

7.1 Perceived Transparency of Business Practices

Business practices are defined by Kaynak (1985) and Quazi (2002) as the assessment of the rate of transparency or fairness of the green activity of the firm. Indeed, to deceive the consumer leading to a loss of confidence, many brands adopt green practices in their activities. These practices can be false advertising, black marketing, etc.

7.2 Willingness to Pay More (Green Value/Price)

Because it requires a specific manufacturing process and because it cannot harm the environment or the population, the green product is considered very expensive compared to a conventional product.

The Bundrage study (2012) shows that while consumers can see added value (green value), they show a willingness to pay more for a green product. To this end, the willingness to pay more is a significant determinant in determining green energy adoption behavior.

8 Conclusion

Green consumption behavior is a field that has attracted much attention from recent research. With the decline in health levels, consumers should consume products that preserve their health. This requires specific consumption behavior. This consumption is said to be sustainable, green or organic. Green consumption thus involves consuming resources at a rate that allows their renewal, polluting only at a rate that the environment can assimilate. It also involves ensuring that the standards of living that individuals enjoy today are not defined at the expense of generations to follow. From an environmental standpoint, the advantages of using green energies are essentially linked to the reduction in the use of fossil fuels and the limitation of CO_2 emissions (Bozorg et al. 2017). Likewise, the shift to renewable energy production has many benefits, including the use of local energy sources, shorter transport distances and reduced losses associated with energy transport. As such, green consumption is a far-reaching and multidimensional global project that requires significant involvement from businesses and consumers. Although government regulations play a major role in encouraging the adoption of green consumption. Other factors are critical to their successful adoption. Studies on green energy adoption behavior have shown that consumer attitude is the variable that explains the consumer's green purchase intention (Bozorg et al. 2017; Solomon 2009). Other research adds the idea that a consumer's attitude is influenced by a set of psychological factors (such as perceived value, influence and social contagion); cultural factors (lifestyle, personality traits and demographics) and economic factors (perceived transparency of business practices and willingness to pay more).

References

Akbar W, Hassan Khurshid S et al (2014) Antecedents affecting customer's purchase intentions towards green products. J Soc Res 5(1):273–289

Baležentis T, Štreimikien˙ D (2019) Sustainability in the electricity sector through advanced technologies: energy mix transition and smart grid technology in China. Ene 12:1142

Barlow J, Maul D (2000) Emotional value: creating strong bonds with your customers. Berrett-Koehler Publishers

BEN MILED-CHERIF H (2001) L'implication du consommateur et ses perspectives stratégiques. Rche et App en Mkg, 16: 66–86

Bloch P (1982) Involvement beyond the purchase process: conceptual issues and empirical investigations. 9:413–417

Bozorg CS, Vaaja MT et al (2017) Target detection distances under different road lighting intensities. Eur Transp Res Rev 9(17)

Caird S, Roy R, Herring H (2008) Improving the energy performance of UK households: results from surveys of consumer adoption and use of low- and zero-carbon technologies. Ener Effic 1(2):149–166

Chandel S, Shrivastva R, Sharma V, Ramasamy P (2016) Overview of the initiatives in renewable energy sector under the national action plan on climate change in India. Renew Sustain Energy Rev 54:866–873

Chen H, Huang Y, Shen H, Chen Y et al (2015) Modeling temporal variations in global residential energy consumption and pollutant emissions. Appl Energy 184:820–829

Crosby Y, Lawrence A, Gill J et al (1981) Consumer/voter behavior in the passage of the Michigan container law. J Mkg 19–32

Diamantopoulos A, Schlegelmilcch B, Sinkovics Rudolf R et al (2003) Can socio-demographics still play a role in profiling green consumers? A review of the evidence and an empirical investigation. J Bus Res 56(6):465–480

Douglas M (2002) The World of goods: towards an anthropology of consumption. Psychology Press

Ek K, Matti S (2014) Valuing the local impacts of a large scale wind power establishment in northern Sweden: public and private preferences toward economic, environmental and sociocultural values. J Environ Plan Manag 58(8):1327–1345

Ellen P, Scholder W et al (1991) The role of perceived consumer effectiveness in motivating environmentally conscious behaviors. J pub po mkg 102:117

Faiers A, Cook M, Neame C (2007) Towards a contemporary approach for understanding consumer behaviour in the context of domestic energy use. Ener Po 35(8):4381–4390

Fennis BM, Pruyn ATH (2007) You are what you wear: brand personality influences on consumer impression formation. J Bus Res 60(6):634–639
Fisk G (1974) Marketing and the ecological crisis. Wisconsin University Madison, New York, Harper & Row
Gale B (1994) Managing customer value. The Free Press, New York
Gatersleben B, White E, Abrahamse W, Jackson T et al (2010) Values and sustainable lifestyles. Archi Sci Rev 53(1):37–50
Gosling P, Ric F et al (1996) Psychologie sociale: approches du sujet social et des relations interpersonnelles. Editions Bréal 1:51
Grunert Suzanne C (1993) Everybody seems concerned about the environment but is this concern reflected in Danish consumers' food choice? Euro Adv Con Res 1:428–433
Gupta S, Ogden DT (2009) To buy or not to buy? A social dilemma perspective on green buying. J Con Mkg 26(6):376–391
Haanpaa L (2007) Consumers' green commitment: indication of a postmodern lifestyle? Int J Con Stu 31(5):478–486
Haas R, Ornetzeder M, Hametner K et al (1999) Socioeconomic aspects of the Austrian 200 kwp-photovoltaic-rooftop programme. Sol Ener 66(3):183–191
Hansla A (2011) Value orientation and framing as determinants of stated willingness to pay for eco-labeled electricity. Ener Effic 4(2):185–192
Hansla A, Gamble A et al (2008) Psychological determinants of attitude towards and willingness to pay for green electricity. Ener Policy 36(2):768–774
Hao Y, Liao H, Wei Y (2015) Is China's carbon reduction target allocation reasonable? An analysis based on carbon intensity convergence. Appl Ener 142:229–239
Hartmann P, Apaolaza-Ibáñez V (2012) Consumer attitude and purchase intention toward green energy brands: the roles of psychological benefits and environmental concern. J Bus Res 65(9):1254–1263
Hartmann P, Ibáñez VA, Sainz JF (2005) Green branding effects on attitude: functional versus emotional positioning strategies. Mark Intell Plan 23(1):9–29
Herbes C, Ramme I (2014) Online marketing of green electricity in Germanyda content analysis of providers' websites. Ene Pol 66:257–266
Hirschman EC (1980) Innovativeness, novelty seeking, and consumer creativity. J Cons Res 7(3):283–295
Holbrook M (1999) Consumer value: a framework for analysis and research. Psychology Press
Holbrook MB (2006) Consumption experience, customer value, and subjective personal introspection: an illustrative photographic essay. J Bus Res 59(6):714–725
Houston M, Rothschild ML (1978) Conceptual and methodological perspectives on involvement, research frontiers in marketing: dialogues and directions In: Jain S (éd) American Marketing Association, Chicago, pp 184 – 187
Ibanez et al (2006) Antecedents of customer loyalty in residential energy markets: service quality, satisfaction, trust and switching costs. Serv Ind J 26(6):633-650
Kaenzig J, Heinzle SL, Wüstenhagen R (2013) Whatever the customer wants, the customer gets? Exploring the gap between consumer preferences and default electricity products in Germany. Ener Po 53:311–322
Kaynak E (1985) Some thoughts on consumerism in developed and less developed countries. Int Mar Rev 2(2):15–30
Kinnear et al (1974) Ecologically concerned consumers: who are they? Ecologically concerned consumers CAN be identified. J Mark 38:20–24
Kondoh K (2009) The challenge of climate change and energy policies for building a sustainable society in Japan. Organ Environ 22(1):52–74
Kostakis I, Sardianou E (2012) Which factors affect the willingness of tourists to pay for renewable energy? Renew Ener 38(1):169–172

Lai AW (1995) Consumer values, product benefits and customer value: a consumption behavior approach. In: Kardes FR, Sujan M (eds) Advances in consumer research 22, éds. Association for Consumer Research, Provo, Utah, 381–388
Lebel L, Lorek S (2008) Enabling sustainable production-consumption systems. Annual Rev Env Res 33:241–275
Lindgreen A, Hingley MK, Grant DB, Morgan RE (2012) Value in business and industrial marketing: past, present, and future. Ind Mark Manag 41(1):207–214
Liu W, Wang C, Mol APJ (2013) Rural public acceptance of renewable energy deployment: the case of Shandong in China. Appl Energy 102:1187–1196
Long TB, Young W, Webber P, Gouldson A, Harwatt H (2014) The impact of domestic energy efficiency retrofit schemes on householder attitudes and behaviours. J Environ Plan Manag 58(10):1–24
Lorenzoni I, Nicholson-Cole S, Whitmarsh L (2007) Barriers perceived to engaging with climate change among the UK public and their policy implications. Glob Environ Change 17(3):445–459
Masini A, Menichetti E (2012) The impact of behavioural factors in the renewable energy investment decision making process: conceptual framework and empirical findings. Energy Policy 40:28–38
Mignon I, Bergek A (2012) Investor motives versus policies to promote investments in renewable electricity production: match or mismatch? In: IST 2012-international conference on sustainability transitions. Copenhagen, Denmark
Nelissen RMA, Meijers MHC (2011) Social benefits of luxury brands as costly signals of wealth and status. Evol Hum Behav 32(5):343–355
Noppers EH, Keizer K, Bolderdijk JW, Steg L (2014) The adoption of sustainable innovations: driven by symbolic and environmental motives. Glob Environ Change 25(1):52–62
Prakash A (2002) Green marketing, public policy and managerial strategies. Bus Strategy Environ 11(5):285–297
Quazi A (2002) Managerial views of consumerism: a two-country comparison. Eur J Mar 36(1/2):36–50
Salazar HA, Oerlemans L, Van Stroe-Biezen S (2013) Social influence on sustainable consumption: evidence from a behavioural experiment. Int J Cons Stud 37(2):172–180
Sangraya and Nayak (2017) Factors influencing buying behaviour of green energy consumer. J Clea Pro 151:393–405
Sarzynski A, Larrieu J, Shrimali G (2012) The impact of state financial incentives on market deployment of solar technology. Ener Po 46:550–557
Sheth J, Newman B, Gross B (1991) Consumption values and market choices: theory and applications. South-Western Publishing Company, Cincinnati
Shove E, Watson M, Spurling N (2015) Conceptualizing connections energy demand, infrastructures and social practices. Eur J Soc Theory 18(3):274–287
Shrimali G, Kniefel J (2011) Are government policies effective in promoting deployment of renewable electricity resources? Ener Po 39(9):4726–4741
Shrimali G, Nelson D, Goel S, Konda C, Kumar R (2013) Renewable deployment in India: financing costs and implications for policy. Ener Po 62:28–43
Solomon M (1983) The role of products as social stimuli: a symbolic interactionism approach. J Consum Res 10(3):319–329
Soonthonsmai V (2001) Predicting intention and behavior to purchase environmentally sound or green products among Thai consumers: An application of the Theory of Reasoned Action. Non published Doctorate thesis, Nova Southeastern University
Sovacool BK, Ratan PL (2012) Conceptualizing the acceptance of wind and solar electricity. Renew Sustain Energy Rev 16(7):5268–5279
Tsoutsos T, Drandaki M, Frantzeskaki N, Iosifidis E, Kiosses I (2009) Sustainable energy planning by using multi-criteria analysis application in the island of Crete. Energy Po 37(5):1587–1600
Upham P, Oltra C, Boso A (2015) Towards a cross-paradigmatic framework of the social acceptance of energy systems. Energy Res Soc Sci 8:100–112

Whtmarsh L, O'neill S (2010) Green identity, green living? The role of proenvironmental self-identity in determining consistency across diverse pro-environmental behaviours. J Env Psy 30(3):305–314
Wiedmann K, Hennigs N, Siebels A (2007) Measuring consumers' luxury value perception: a cross-cultural framework. Acad Mark Sci 7(7):333–361
Wüstenhagen R, Bilharz M (2006) Green energy market development in Germany: effective public policy and emerging customer demand. Energy pol 34(13):1681–1696
Wüstenhagen R, Wolsink M, Bürer MJ (2007) Social acceptance of renewable energy innovation: an introduction to the concept. Energy Pol 35(5):2683–2691
Xingang Z, Jieyu W, Xiaomeng L Pingkuo L (2012) China's wind, biomass and solar power generation: What the situation tells us? Renew Sustain Energy Rev 16:6173–6182
Yang Y, Solgaard HS, Haider W (2015) Value seeking, price sensitive, or green? Analyzing preference heterogeneity among residential energy consumers in Denmark. Energy Res Soc Sci 6:15–28
Zaichkowsky JL (1985) Measuring the involvement construct. J Con Res 12:341–352
Zarnikau J (2003) Consumer demand for "green power" and energy efficiency. Energy Pol 31(15):1661–1672
Zeithaml V (1988) Consumer perceptions of price, quality, and value: a means-end model and synthesis of evidence. J Mark 2–22

Sihem Ben Saad is an Assistant Professor of Marketing at the Carthage Business School of the University of Tunis Carthage (UTC), Tunisia. She holds a Ph.D. degree in Marketing from the Institute of Higher Business Studies of Carthage (IHEC Carthage). Before joining UTC, she held faculty positions at the Higher School of Communications of Tunis (Supcom Tunis), Higher Institute of Computer Science (ISI Tunis), and Higher Institute of Technological Studies of Communications of Tunis (ISET'COM). Her research interests include digital marketing and child behavior. Dr. Ben Saad taught a variety of courses such as introduction to marketing, consumer behavior, project management, entrepreneurship and corporate culture. She presented papers at several national and international conferences such as the French Association of Marketing (AFM) and the Tunisian Association of Marketing (ATM).

On the Role of Financial Development in Access to Electricity

Soumaya Ben Khelifa and Sonia Arsi

Abstract Over the last decade, the world has been experiencing considerable economic and financial development along with a rising level of energy demand (Zafar et al. 2019). Within this framework, this chapter investigate the nexus between financial development and access to electricity across the UfM countries, while considering the type of population (rural or urban population). The results display a significant effect of financial development on the access to electricity for the overall population. However, the effect seems to be neutral while spreading the analysis over rural and urban populations.

Keywords Financial development · Access to electricity · Rural · Urban · UfM countries

1 Introduction

The 2030 envision of the United Nations, defined as 2030 Agenda for Sustainable Development, consists of achieving several goals, known as Sustainable Development Goals (SDGs). Within this context, the access to energy is a key element to development. Particularly, this agenda includes reaching "a universal electricity access goal by 2030".

The report "World Energy Outlook 2020" of International Energy Agency (IEA) reported that the access to electricity increased from 73% in 2000 to 90% in 2019 at a worldwide level, with 85% and 96% for rural and urban populations, respectively.

Indeed, the access to electricity is a challenging concern due to its matter in the environmental and social contexts. Shyu (2014) stated that the access to electricity should be prioritized by politicians and policymakers as it will ensure fairness between individuals. Equally, Alam et al. (2018) found that the access to electricity

S. B. Khelifa (✉) · S. Arsi
University of Carthage-Carthage Business School, Tunis, Tunisia
e-mail: soumaya.benkhelifa@utctunisie.com

S. Arsi
e-mail: Sonia.arsi@utctunisie.com

S. Goutte et al. (eds.), *Advances in Managing Energy and Climate Risks*, Lecture Notes in Energy 82, https://doi.org/10.1007/978-3-030-71403-1_7

contributes to labor productivity across 56 developing countries from 1991 to 2013. The access to electricity is a key issue. However, one can here shed light on the role of financial development which is crucial in an "energy–growth-environment" (Iorember et al. 2020). Thus, analyzing its impact on the access to electricity can provide handy insights on this issue.

This chapter is organized as follows. Section 1 relates the theoretical background. Section 2 describes the data and Sect. 3 defines the methodology. The results are depicted in Sect. 4. Finally, Sect. 5 wraps up.

2 Literature Review

The access to electricity is still a prevalent issue across academicians and researchers, as it takes on a whole significance while considering the several factors related to the access to electricity. Among the most notable work, we can mention Kanagawa and Nakata (2008) that studied the access to electricity in rural regions of Assam state in India. The outcome displayed that advanced infrastructures, a well-studied government policy and country's capacity for international cooperation increases the accessibility to electricity. Furthermore, Zhang et al. (2019) examined the socio-economic development factors impacting the access to electricity in 48 developing countries over the period 2005–2014. The authors found that banking sector, education, income, access to developed networking services, and industrial infrastructure move jointly with the access to electricity.

However, interesting work tend to specifically study the linkage between financial development and access to electricity. Sadorsky (2010) showed that financial development, measured through several proxies, boosts the demand for energy across the 22 emerging countries studied over the period 1990–2006. Equally, Sekantsi and Timuno (2017) investigates the factors affecting the electricity demand in Botswana from 1981 to 2011. The outcome displayed that economic growth, a thriving industrial sector and financial development contribute to boost the electricity consumption. However, it seems that urbanization has a positive effect only on the long-run. Recently, Rakpho et al. (2020) underlined that financial development is positively linked to the accessibility to electricity and renewable energy in 16 Asian countries from 2000 to 2016. This can be explained by the flows being available for investment in the energy sector. And, Liu and Li (2020) found that financial development increases urban electricity consumption through the industrial structure in 278 Chinese cities from 2005 to 2016.

Following this framework, researches tend to focus on a particular region or a panel of countries without considering the difference between the access to electricity per rural or urban population. In order to overcome this gap, this chapter contributes to the existing literature an examines the effect of financial development on electricity access in the Union for Mediterranean countries (UfM countries hereafter), while considering macro-economic variables and distinguishing between rural and urban populations. Besides, compared to other studies that tend to pick up each financial development's proxy apart, this investigation considers a weighted index to proxy financial development using a principal component analysis (PCA).

3 Data

All data were collected from the World Development Indicators (2019) of the World Bank and we use panel data of the UfM countries included in the World Bank database, ranging from 2000 to 2018. In order to construct the Financial Development Index (FDI hereafter), we use the following indicators: Domestic Credit to Private Sector, Total Reserves, Commercial Bank Branches (per 100,000 adults), Automated Teller Machines (ATMs) (per 100,000 adults).

The access to electricity is measured by the following indicators: access to electricity as percentage of the overall population, and access to electricity as percentage of urban and rural populations. The here below table summarizes the variables to be used and their corresponding descriptions.

Table. Data Elaboration and Sources

Variables	Description	Source
DCPS	Domestic credit to private sector (% of GDP)	World development indicators
Reserves	Total reserves (includes gold, current US$)	
CBB	Commercial bank branches (per 100,000 adults)	
ATMs	Automated teller machines (ATMs) (per 100,000 adults)	
AcElec	Access to electricity (% of population)	
AcElec rural	Access to electricity, rural (% of rural population)	
AcElec urban	Access to electricity, urban (% of urban population)	
AFF	Agriculture, forestry, and fishing, value added (% of GDP)	
Rule	Rule of Law	
Internet	Individuals using the Internet (% of population)	

4 Methodology

To construct the Financial Development Index (FDI), we use the methodology followed by prior studies as the work of Cámara and Tuesta (2014) and Sha'ban et al. (2019). In the first step, each indicator is computed as:

$$I_{i,F} = \frac{V_i - m_i}{M_i - m_i} \tag{1}$$

where V_i is the actual value of the indicator i, m_i is the minimum value of indicator i, M_i is the maximum value of indicator i, and $I_{i,F}$ is the standardised value of indicator i of the index F.

In a second step, the PCA method is used in order to aggregate each indicator to the index. Following Cámara and Tuesta (2014), we calculate the estimator of the financial development index F_i using the weighted averages:

$$FDI_i = \frac{\sum_{j,k=1}^{p} \lambda_j P_{ki}}{\sum_{j,k=1}^{p} \lambda_j} \tag{2}$$

where $P_k = X^* \lambda_j$; λ_j is the variance of the kth principal component, and X represents the indicators matrix.

$$\begin{aligned}\text{Financial Development Index (FDI)} &= (w_1 \times \text{Indicator}_1) \\ &+ (w_2 \times \text{Indicator}_2) + (w_3 \times \text{Indicator}_3) + (w_4 \times \text{Indicator}_4)\end{aligned} \tag{3}$$

where w is the weight related to the indicator in the principal component analysis.

Once we construct the FDI, we investigate the association between financial development and access to electricity using the following model in a panel setup.

$$AcElec_{i,t} = FDI_{i,t-1} + AFF_{i,t-1} + Internet_{\ i,t-1} + Rule_{\ i,t-1} + \varepsilon_{i,t}$$

Furthermore, we consider the type of population (whether rural or urban population). Hence, the suggested specifications are shown below:

$$AcElec\ rural_{i,t} = FDI_{i,t-1} + AFF_{i,t-1} + Internet_{\ i,t-1} + Rule_{\ i,t-1} + \varepsilon_{i,t}$$
$$AcElec\ urban_{i,t} = FDI_{i,t-1} + AFF_{i,t-1} + Internet_{\ i,t-1} + Rule_{\ i,t-1} + \varepsilon_{i,t}$$

5 Empirical Results

5.1 Descriptive Statistics

Table 1 reports the descriptive statistics of the available data of financial development proxies employed to build the index (panel 1) and that of related to the determinants of access to electricity (panel 2). The results suggest a high variation in the level of financial development between countries. On an average, the domestic credit to private sector for the UfM countries is 82.31995% of GDP, whereas the total reserves are around 4.17E+10$. The average number of commercial bank branches and ATMs is 30.03715 and 71.13147 per 100,000 adults, respectively.

Table 1 Summary statistics

Panel 1: Financial development indicators					
Variable	Number of observations	Mean	Standard deviation	Minimum	Maximum
Domestic credit to private sector (% of GDP)	412	82.31995	44.61533	13.71548	255.3103
Total reserves (includes gold, current US$)	412	4.17E+10	5.18E+10	2.07E+08	2.49E+11
Commercial bank branches (per 100,000 adults)	412	30.03715	18.95541	1.433379	103.7535
Automated teller machines (ATMs) (per 100,000 adults)	412	71.13147	39.70209	4.240259	194.6011
Panel 2: Determinants: Access to electricity					
Access to electricity	373	98.75179	8.152441	36.43715	100
Agriculture, forestry, and fishing, value added	373	4.087104	4.148085	0.2140494	21.73921
Rule of Law	373	0.7547141	0.8309227	−0.9984549	2.100273
Individuals using the Internet	372	64.74285	20.1659	4.5	98.1367

Table 2 Composition of the financial development index

Index	Indicators	Normalized weights
Financial development index	Domestic credit to private sector (% of GDP)	0.313
	Total reserves (includes gold, current US$)	0.280
	Commercial bank branches (per 100,000 adults)	0.234
	Automated teller machines (ATMs) (per 100,000 adults)	0.173

5.2 *Normalized Weights*

Table 2 shows the computed weights for each proxy in the financial development index. The indicator for domestic credit has the highest weight (0.313), followed by total reserves, commercial bank branches, and ATMs, at 0.280, 0.234, and 0.173, respectively. These weights are obtained from Eq. (3) and normalized so that their sum is equal to 1. Hence, domestic credit to private sector is the most important indicator in explaining financial development in UfM countries.

5.3 *Financial Development Index*

Table 3 reports the list of the UfM countries ranked by the level of financial development from the highest to the lowest for each year. The findings suggest that high incomes economies like Spain, Portugal, Cyprus, Italy, Germany, and Luxembourg are ranked in the top ten during the overall period 2008–2018. In fact, a high score on FDI rankings indicates that developed countries have the most developed financial system. However, the last ten economies, at the bottom of the ranking are upper and lower middle-income countries like Tunisia, Jordon, and Egypt. These countries perform poorly in financial development terms (Table 3).

Figure 1 shows a small downward trend in FDI for UfM countries during the period ranging from 2008 to 2018.

5.4 *Financial Development and Access to Electricity*

Results presented in Table 5 yield a number of interesting findings. Our estimation in column (1) indicates that Financial Development Index is positively and significantly related to access to electricity for all populations. Agriculture, forestry, and fishing indicator has also a positive and significant correlation with access to electricity.

Table 3 Index of financial development ranking (2008–2018)

Rank	FDI2008	FDI2009	FDI2010	FDI2011	FDI2012	FDI2013	FDI2014	FDI2015	FDI2016	FDI2017	FDI2018
1	Spain	Spain	Spain	Spain	Spain	Spain	Spain	Spain	France	France	France
2	Portugal	Portugal	Portugal	Portugal	Italy	Portugal	Italy	France	Spain	Germany	Italy
3	United Kingdom	Denmark	Italy	Italy	Portugal	United Kingdom	Portugal	Italy	Italy	Italy	Spain
4	Cyprus	United Kingdom	United Kingdom	Germany	Germany	Italy	France	Cyprus	Germany	Spain	Luxembourg
5	Denmark	Cyprus	Cyprus	United Kingdom	France	France	Germany	Germany	Portugal	Cyprus	Portugal
6	Italy	Italy	France	France	United Kingdom	Germany	Cyprus	Portugal	Cyprus	Portugal	Denmark
7	Luxembourg	Germany	Germany	Cyprus	Cyprus	Cyprus	Denmark	Luxembourg	Luxembourg	Luxembourg	Israel
8	France	France	Denmark	Denmark	Denmark	Denmark	Luxembourg	Denmark	Denmark	Denmark	Poland
9	Germany	Luxembourg	Luxembourg	Luxembourg	Luxembourg	Luxembourg	Austria	Austria	Poland	Israel	Czech Republic
10	Bulgaria	Bulgaria	Bulgaria	Israel	Israel	Israel	Israel	Turkey	Israel	Czech Republic	Cyprus
11	Ireland	Ireland	Israel	Bulgaria	Bulgaria	Turkey	Turkey	Israel	Turkey	Poland	Austria
12	Netherlands	Netherlands	Ireland	Greece	Poland	Bulgaria	Sweden	Bulgaria	Austria	Turkey	Bulgaria
13	Belgium	Sweden	Greece	Sweden	Sweden	Sweden	Bulgaria	Sweden	Sweden	Austria	Turkey
14	Greece	Malta	Netherlands	Netherlands	Greece	Poland	Poland	Poland	Bulgaria	Sweden	Croatia
15	Malta	Belgium	Sweden	Malta	Netherlands	Croatia	Croatia	Croatia	Croatia	Bulgaria	Montenegro
16	Slovenia	Slovenia	Slovenia	Poland	Turkey	Greece	Netherlands	Belgium	Lebanon	Croatia	Netherlands
17	Sweden	Israel	Malta	Ireland	Austria	Austria	Belgium	Greece	Belgium	Lebanon	Greece
18	Austria	Greece	Belgium	Austria	Croatia	Netherlands	Greece	Lebanon	Czech Republic	Belgium	Morocco
19	Israel	Croatia	Poland	Slovenia	Malta	Belgium	Lebanon	Netherlands	Netherlands	Netherlands	Malta
20	Croatia	Austria	Croatia	Croatia	Belgium	Malta	Malta	Malta	Greece	Greece	Slovenia
21	Montenegro	Poland	Austria	Belgium	Slovenia	Ireland	Algeria	Czech Republic	Malta	Montenegro	Bosnia and Herzegovina
22	Estonia	Estonia	Latvia	Lebanon	Ireland	Algeria	Ireland	Montenegro	Montenegro	Malta	Slovak Republic
23	Poland	Montenegro	Estonia	Turkey	Lebanon	Lebanon	Slovenia	Slovenia	Morocco	Morocco	Romania
24	Romania	Romania	Lebanon	Algeria	Algeria	Slovenia	Montenegro	Algeria	Slovenia	Slovenia	Ireland
25	Hungary	Lebanon	Turkey	Latvia	Romania	Montenegro	Czech Republic	Morocco	Romania	Romania	Finland
26	Turkey	Hungary	Romania	Romania	Montenegro	Czech Republic	Romania	Romania	Ireland	Bosnia and Herzegovina	Hungary
27	Bosnia and Herzegovina	Algeria	Montenegro	Montenegro	Morocco	Romania	Morocco	Ireland	Bosnia and Herzegovina	Slovak Republic	Estonia
28	Czech Republic	Bosnia and Herzegovina	Algeria	Hungary	Latvia	Morocco	Bosnia and Herzegovina	Bosnia and Herzegovina	Slovak Republic	Tunisia	Algeria
29	Finland	Czech Republic	Hungary	Estonia	Czech Republic	Bosnia and Herzegovina	Finland	Slovak Republic	Algeria	Ireland	Latvia
30	Slovak Republic	Finland	Morocco	Morocco	Estonia	Hungary	Hungary	Tunisia	Tunisia	Algeria	Lithuania
31	Jordan	Jordan	Lithuania	Czech Republic	Hungary	Latvia	Estonia	Estonia	Estonia	Estonia	Albania
32	Tunisia	Slovak Republic	Czech Republic	Finland	Bosnia and Herzegovina	Finland	Slovak Republic	Finland	Finland	Finland	Egypt, Arab Rep.
33	Egypt, Arab Rep.	Tunisia	Finland	Bosnia and Herzegovina	Finland	Estonia	Tunisia	Hungary	Jordan	Hungary	Mauritania
34		Egypt, Arab Rep.	Bosnia and Herzegovina	Slovak Republic	Slovak Republic	Slovak Republic	Latvia	Latvia	Hungary	Latvia	
35			Jordan	Jordan	Tunisia	Tunisia	Jordan	Jordan	Latvia	Lithuania	
36			Slovak Republic	Tunisia	Jordan	Jordan	Lithuania	Lithuania	Lithuania	Albania	
37			Tunisia	Lithuania	Lithuania	Lithuania	Albania	Albania	Albania	Egypt, Arab Rep.	
38			Egypt, Arab Rep.	Egypt, Arab Rep.	Albania	Albania	Egypt, Arab Rep.	Egypt, Arab Rep.	Egypt, Arab Rep.	Mauritania	
39				Mauritania	Egypt, Arab Rep.	Egypt, Arab Rep.	Mauritania	Mauritania	Mauritania		
40					Mauritania	Mauritania					

Consistent with our expectation, technology measured by individuals using internet is positively and significantly associated with access to electricity. Finally, we note a positive and significant relationship between rule of law and access to electricity.

Results reported in columns (2) and (3) show that financial development do not significantly covariate with access to electricity for both rural and urban populations, implying that belonging to rural or urban area don't does not make the effect of financial development greater or weaker.

Table 4 Correlation matrix

	Financial development index	Agriculture, forestry, and fishing, value added	Individuals using the internet	Rule of law
Financial development index	1	–	–	–
Agriculture, forestry, and fishing, value added	0.0632	1	–	–
Individuals using the internet	0.2237	0.0259	1	–
Rule of law	0.0376	0.0528	0.1032	1

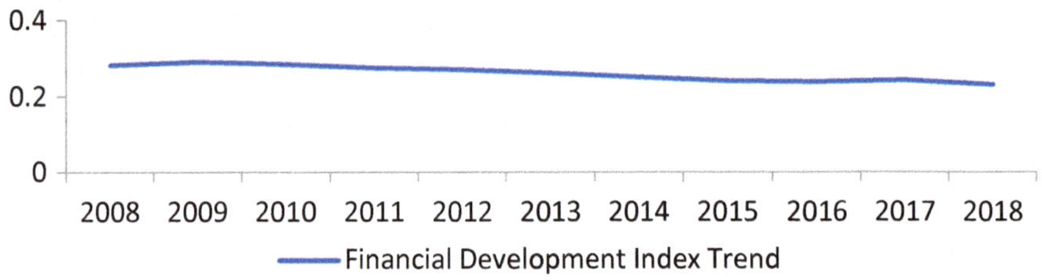

Fig. 1 Financial development index trend

Table 5 Determinants of financial development index

Dependent variable	AcElec	AcElec rural	AcElec urban
$FDI_{(t-1)}$	1.98093*	1.032777	1.101003
	(1.89)	(0.20)	(0.82)
Agriculture, forestry, and fishing$_{(t-1)}$	0.2652831***	−1.688782***	−0.3698106***
	(4.63)	(−8.42)	(−6.94)
Internet$_{(t-1)}$	0.0168829***	0.1622575***	0.0681088***
	(3.77)	(3.89)	(5.13)
Rule of law$_{(t-1)}$	0.5806785**	−5.836725***	−1.785509***
	(2.33)	(−5.06)	(−5.46)
C	95.1879***	98.86251***	97.65013***
	(68.65)	(30.98)	(104.75)
Observations	372	370	372
Adjusted R-squared	9.45%	27.51%	27.92%

6 Conclusion

This chapter investigates the role of financial development on access to electricity across the UfM countries from 2008 to 2018. The outputs show the significance of financial development for overall population to access to electricity. However, the analysis breakdown over rural and urban populations displays a neutral effect of financial development on any ability to access to electricity. Furthermore, common factors seem to affect the access to electricity, whether considering overall, rural or urban populations, but in different ways. A thriving agriculture, forestry, and fishing sector and a good obedience to laws contributes to facilitate the access to electricity to overall population, which is the reverse case if the population is spread into rural and urban. Additionally, as individuals use extensively internet, the access to electricity is smoothed for all populations. Following these results, policymakers should encourage investments on electricity or even its alternative sources, like renewable and solar energy (Sekantsi and Timuno 2017). This can ensure fairness vis-à-vis both rural and urban populations. Equally, the decision makers in the agriculture, forestry, and fishing sector should review and design their policies in the way to be adapted by urban and rural populations. Besides, rule of law has to be respected.

Our study includes drawbacks. The Financial Development Index (FDI) is constructed upon the available data. The accessibility to additional indicators can help to establish another index and may lead to different results. Equally, the analysis was limited to UfM countries and it can be extended to further countries.

Further investigation can try to bridge the prementioned gaps. First, it can rethink the step up of the FDI index following the available data. Second, considering another sample of countries may yield to new findings.

References

Alam MS, Miah MD, Hammoudeh S, Tiwari AK (2018) The nexus between access to electricity and labour productivity in developing countries. Energy Policy 122:715–726. https://doi.org/10.1016/j.enpol.2018.08.009

Cámara N, Tuesta D (2014) Measuring Financial inclusion: a multidimensional index. BBVA Research Working Paper, 14/26

Iorember PT, Goshit GG, Dabwor DT (2020) Testing the nexus between renewable energy consumption and environmental quality in Nigeria: the role of broad-based financial development. Afr Dev Rev 30:163–175. https://doi.org/10.1111/1467-8268.12425

Kanagawa M, Nakata T (2008) Assessment of access to electricity and the socio-economic impacts in rural areas of developing countries. Energy Policy 36:2016–2029. https://doi.org/10.1016/j.enpol.2008.01.041

Liu S, Li H (2020) Does financial development increase urban electricity consumption? Evidence from spatial and heterogeneity analysis. Sustainability 12. https://doi.org/10.3390/su12177011

Rakpho P, Yamaka W, Puttachai W, Maneejuk P (2020) Role of financial development for solving the energy insecurity in Asia. Singap Econ Rev. https://doi.org/10.1142/S0217590820430018

Sadorsky P (2010) The impact of financial development on energy consumption in emerging economies. Energy Policy 38:2528–2535. https://doi.org/10.1016/j.enpol.2009.12.048

Sekantsi LP, Timuno S (2017) Electricity consumption in Botswana: the role of financial development, industrialisation and urbanization. Rev Econ Bus Stud 10(1):75–102. https://doi.org/10.1515/rebs-2017-0049

Sha'ban M, Girardone C, Sarkisyan, A (2019) Cross-country variation in financial inclusion: a global perspective. Eur J Finan 26(4):1–22. https://doi.org/10.1080/1351847X.2019.1686709

Shyu CW (2014) Ensuring access to electricity and minimum basic electricity needs as a goal for the post-MDG development agenda after 2015. Energy Sustain Dev 19:24–38. https://doi.org/10.1016/j.esd.2013.11.005

World Developement Indicators (2019) https://databank.worldbank.org/

Zafar MW, Zaidi SAH, Sinha A, Gedikli A, Hou F (2019) The role of stock market and banking sector development, and renewable energy consumption in carbon emissions: insights from G-7 and N-11 countries. Resour Policy 62:427–436. https://doi.org/10.1016/j.resourpol.2019.05.003

Zhang T, Shi X, Zhang D, Xiao J (2019) Socio-economic development and electricity access in developing economies: a long-run model averaging approach. Energy Policy 132:223–231. https://doi.org/10.1016/j.enpol.2019.05.031

Soumaya Ben Khelifa is Assistant Professor in Finance at Carthage Business School, University of Tunis Carthage. She holds a Ph.D. in Finance from IHEC Carthage, Tunisia in April 2016. Her areas of research are: Asset Pricing, Hedge Funds, International Finance, Market Finance, Financial Inclusion and Energy Market.

Sonia Arsi holds a Ph.D. (finance) from IHEC Carthage, Tunisia. She is currently an assistant professor of finance at Carthage Business School, University of Tunis Carthage; she teaches topics of international finance, asset pricing, corporate finance, and treasury management. Her research interests include behavioral finance, derivatives, commodities, and international finance.

The Impact of COVID-19 Pandemic on Renewable Energy and Commodity Markets

Yosra Ghabri and Ahmed Ayadi

Abstract The aim of this chapter is to investigate the reaction of renewable energy and commodity markets to the adverse shocks of Covid-19 pandemic. To this purpose, we use time-varying parameter vector autoregression (TVP-VAR) approach during the period from 02 January 2020 to 17 April 2020, while distinguishing between two sub-periods: before and after the announcement of the pandemic. The results show that the returns of both European renewable energy index and major precious metals (Gold, Silver, and Platinum) have increased after the announcement of the pandemic. However, except Soybean, the agriculture commodities (Corn and Wheat) did not respond to Covid-19 shocks during the same period. Moreover, our findings reveal that the renewable energy is the most volatile market, yet the agriculture industry is the least volatile. These results support the safe haven capability of Gold and suggest the hedging ability of some precious metals and agriculture commodities in periods of the pandemic. However, the implications of the Covid-19 pandemic on renewable energy and commodity markets are expected to persist in the long term.

Keywords Covid 19 pandemic · Renewable energy · Precious metals · Agricultural commodities · TVP-VAR

1 Introduction

The coronavirus (Covid-19) outbreak has driven down the prices of major commodities (World Bank's *Commodity Markets Outlook* 2020). The stop of global economic activities and the large drop in demand during the outbreak have negatively affected most energy and metals commodities. Crude oil which is associated with transportation has experienced an unprecedented collapse, trading at negative prices in April

Y. Ghabri (✉)
University of Tunis Carthage-Carthage Business School, Tunis, Tunisia
e-mail: yosra.ghabri@utctunisie.com

A. Ayadi
Center of Research for Energy and Climate Change (CRECC)-Paris School of Business, IHEC Carthage, University Paris 8, Tunis, Tunisia
e-mail: ahmed_ayedi93@live.fr

S. Goutte et al. (eds.), *Advances in Managing Energy and Climate Risks*, Lecture Notes in Energy 82, https://doi.org/10.1007/978-3-030-71403-1_8

2020. Industrial metals are also affected by the shutdown of key industries and the slowing demand; and are expected to decline 13% during 2020. Less affected by mitigation measures, agriculture commodities have faced smaller declines in prices in comparison to energy commodities.

On March 11th 2020, the World Health Organization (WHO) has declared the recent Covid-19 disease as a pandemic (WHO 2020; Gupta et al. 2020). In order to fight against the rapid spread of Covid-19, governments worldwide have adopted several mitigation measures with restrictions in traveling and complete lockdowns in many countries. This global pandemic has caused an unprecedented shock to economic activities (Gautam 2020; Meninno and Wolff 2020). Covid-19 has also caused a simultaneous supply and demand shocks slowing down the trade flows and creating distortions in international supply chains (Baldwin and Tomiura 2020). The demand and supply shocks are followed by a significant decline in commodity markets in short time duration (Mann 2020; Baldwin and di Munro 2020). Since January 2020, major energy and non-energy commodity prices have faced a declining trend. However, the consequences of these shocks are widely varying on different energy and non-energy commodity markets. Due to travel bans and restrictions and the outrageous collapse in the demand, the oil market has experienced the steepest decline in prices. Renewable energy stocks and metal prices have also dropped, while the price fall is less than oil prices. Due to its indirect relationship with economic activities, the agriculture commodity market is the least influenced by this current pandemic because food security is a prime concern.

Although, there is a growing literature focusing on the effect of Covid -19 on different financial markets (Bakas and Triantafyllou 2020; Salisu et al. 2020a; Sharif et al. 2020; Corbet et al. 2020; Conlon and McGee 2020; Wang et al. 2020), the interaction between Covid-19 cases, renewable energy and commodity markets is not widely analyzed yet. The uncertainty surrounding the ongoing pandemic is motivating us to examine the reaction of renewable energy and commodity markets to the outspread of Covid-19. More precisely, this chapter contributes to the previous studies by focusing on the impact of the pandemic shocks on the stock returns of European renewable clean energy index and those of various precious metals and agricultural commodities. We consider Platinum, Silver, Gold and Aluminum as precious metals and Corn, Wheat and Soybeans as agricultural commodities.

Using a time-varying parameter vector autoregression (TVP-VAR) approach, our findings show an increase in the returns of renewable clean energy stocks and most precious metals after the announcement of Covid-19 as a pandemic except for Aluminum. However, agriculture commodities (Corn and Wheat) did not respond to the pandemic, apart Soybeans which reacted positively as for Gold. Furthermore, the stochastic volatility shows that renewable clean energy stocks are the most volatile and agricultural commodities are the least volatile after the announcement of the Pandemic. The results of the variance decompositions indicate that renewable energy reacted the most, followed by precious metals and agriculture commodities which reacted the least. These results support the safe haven properties for Gold and document the hedging characteristics of some precious metals and agriculture commodities in turmoil periods.

The rest of the chapter is arranged as follows: Sect. 2 reviews the related studies. Section 3 describes the dataset and the adopted methodology. Section 4 discusses the empirical results and Sect. 5 concludes.

2 Effect of Covid-19 on Non-Energy and Commodity Markets

2.1 *Effect on Renewable and Clean Energy*

Due to supply chain delays, energy demand drop, tax stock markets problems and government incentives delay, the renewable and clean energy transition were affected by the Covid-19 pandemic (Birol 2020).

The global outbreak has caused a decline on the renewable energy global supply chain followed by a significant reduction in renewable energy investments (Emma 2020). For instance, due to the stringent containment measures, several companies have decided to stop the installation of wind turbines and others have stopped in the delivery phase (McPhee 2020). Furthermore, due to Covid-19, the renewable energy investment estimates for 2020 in the solar industry declined by 28% because workers have been dismissed, in addition to equipment and supply chain delay and construction delays (SEIA 2020a). By contrast, renewables in global electricity supply were resilient during Covid-19 outbreak reaching 28% since January 2020. Despite this resilience, the renewable power sources' growth are anticipated to decline after the first quarter, because of lockdown measures, supply chain disruptions, and financing challenges. In addition to that, the collapse of oil prices is making clean energy technologies less competitive. Meanwhile, renewable and clean energy investment has been more resilient than fossil energy in the first quarter of 2020.

Many of the world's largest renewable energy construction projects like wind turbine and solar panel are located in China. Travel restrictions and country lockdowns are delaying delivery of key components, disrupting supply chains and increasing costs.

2.2 *Effect on Precious and Industrial Metals*

During Covid-19 outbreak, most industrial metals have witnessed a drop in prices but substantially less than oil markets collapse. Due to the global economic activities slowdown, copper and zinc prices experienced the largest fall since January (commodity market outlook, 2020). China represents more than half of the global demand of metals. Due to mitigation measures, 15% of the copper and 20% of zinc mining activities are operating at lower capacities influencing the supply of metals. Whereas, iron ore supply in Brazil and Australia are less influenced because they are remote operational and highly automated. Due to uncertain situation and safe-haven capability, Gold prices significantly increased during the early stages of Covid-19 pandemic and then observed some fluctuations in March 2020 to cover margin calls. Regarding other precious metals, platinum and silver prices have fallen substantially in March and remained at a lower level in April and then experienced a small recovery. More than half of the platinum supply in the world is produced from South Africa and major platinum demand are impacted by reduced automobile production (World Bank 2019). The stoppage of mining activities has affected platinum metal prices.

2.3 *Effect on Agriculture Commodities*

Due to its indirect association with economic activities, agriculture commodity markets are so far less affected by the Covid-19 outbreak and observed some minor declines in prices at the beginning of the 2020. However, natural rubber faced a sharp fall because of its use in transportation sector. As production levels are at high records, prices of staple foods are remaining stable. Whereas, disruptions in production and distribution and labor availability may affect agriculture commodity prices. This modest decline in prices reveals that agriculture commodities demand is lower in comparison to industrial commodities. Corn and soybeans which are used for biofuels production were affected by decreased gasoline production and oil prices. Besides, labor availability is a major concern for agriculture activities particularly for the production of vegetables and fruit products.

3 Literature Review

Numerous studies have examined the impact of pandemic on macroeconomic activities as financial markets (Elnahas et al. 2018; Chen et al. 2018; Bloom et al. 2018), and banking and insurance (Leoni 2013). Previous research findings show a strong interaction between pandemic and macroeconomic activities and reveal high economic cost due to pandemic. The outspread of Covid-19 pandemic has attracted a lot of attention from policymakers, investors and researchers in order to understand how and whether the Covid-19 crisis affects financial markets and investors' expectations. Understanding the impact of the current Covid-19 outbreak is not only crucial for investors to formulate the appropriate strategy for their investments, but also significant for governments worldwide to anticipate the severity of the situation and deal with the expected fluctuation in financial markets.

According to Goodell (2020), the coronavirus is defined as an unprecedented global crisis affecting all economic activities. As for other financial markets, the emergence of Covid-19 pandemic has affected energy and commodity markets (e.g.,

Corbet et al. 2020; Bakas and Triantafyllou 2020; Wang et al 2020; Salisu et al. 2020a, b; among others).

The majority of previous studies focusing on agricultural commodities investigate the relationship between the return and volatility of crude oil or energy prices and agriculture commodities (e.g., Serra 2011; Reboredo 2012; Koirala et al. 2015; Kang et al. 2017; Dahl et al. 2019; Yahya et al. 2019; Yip et al. 2020; Tiwari et al. 2020). The findings support a significant relationship between agricultural commodities and energy markets, specifically oil while other studies document the opposite. For instance, Koirala et al. (2015) investigate the interaction between corn, soybean and energy commodities and find a higher volatility transmission between the different markets. Further, Kang et al. (2017) examine the return and volatility spillover between six commodity futures indices and document a positive correlation between the returns of commodity futures markets. In the same line, Dahl et al. (2019) examine the spillover effect among crude oil and agricultural commodities and find a bidirectional and an asymmetric flow of information between crude oil and agricultural commodities. However, Cabrera and Schulz (2016) study the association between agricultural and energy markets and find that energy markets do not increase agricultural prices volatility.

Bakas and Triantafyllou (2018) investigate how and whether the volatility of energy, agricultural, and metals commodities are affected by macroeconomic events. The results show that macroeconomic events have a positive effect on the volatility of these markets. Further, Prokopczuk et al. (2019) examine the relationship between economic uncertainty and livestock, energy, agricultural and metals commodity markets and find a strong association between commodity market volatility and economic uncertainty.

When it comes to the recent studies focusing on the effect of Covid-19 pandemic on different financial markets, the increasing literature are contributing gradually. For instance, Bakas and Triantafyllou (2020) examine the impact of Covid-19 on the volatility of two commodity prices god and crude oil. The authors show a significantly negative response of oil market to Covid-19 pandemic; however the Gold market exhibits a positive and less significant relationship. In the same vein, applying a panel VAR model, Salisu et al. (2020a) document a positive interaction between Covid-19 fear and commodity returns. Using a time frequency domain, Sharif et al. (2020) analyze the connectedness between oil, stock markets and Covid-19. Corbet et al. (2020) study the contagion effects of the global pandemic on several cryptocurrencies and Gold. Similarly, Conlon and McGee (2020) examine the safe-haven ability of cryptocurrencies against equity markets volatility. Besides, Wang et al. (2020) investigate the impact of the pandemic on the cross-correlations between agricultural futures markets and crude oil and find a strong correlation between sugar and oil.

While the existing studies have focused on the linkages between stocks and crude oil under Covid-19, they paid little attention on the interaction between Covid-19, renewable energy and commodity markets. To fill this gap, this chapter provides new insights into the impact of Covid-19 pandemic on renewable energy and commodity markets namely precious metals and agricultural commodities. Specifically, this chapter attempts to understand the reaction of renewable clean energy sector, precious metals and agricultural commodities to the outspread of this global pandemic.

4 Data and Methodology

Our study employed daily data on Covid-19 global cases and daily closing prices of the European Renewable Energy Index (ERIX). As for precious metals, we used the daily closing prices for Platinum, Aluminum, Gold and Silver. Then, we collected daily closing price of Corn, Wheat and Soybean for agriculture commodities. The period of study is spanning from January 2nd, 2020 to April 17th, 2020; divided into two sub-period: (1) from January 2st to March 10th, before the announcement of the pandemic, and (2) from March 11th to April 17th 2020, after the announcement of the pandemic by WHO. The data for the renewable energy stocks, precious metals and agriculture commodities prices are obtained from Bloomberg. Covid-19 global cases data are collected from the daily reports published by the WHO. All the variables are used in the first differences.

In order to examine the time-varying effects of Covid-19 shocks on renewable clean energy, precious metals, and agriculture commodities returns, we used the TVP-VAR with Stochastic Volatility, presented by Primiceri (2005) and Del Negro and Primiceri (2015). The model is presented as follows:

$$\mathrm{y_t = X_t\beta_t + A_t^{-1}\Sigma_t u_t}$$

where y_t is a $(k\,x\,2)$ matrices holding the independent variables, X_t is a $(k\,x\,2)$ matrices holding the 1 lagged observations of the independent variables and u_t is the error term. The coefficients β_t and the parameters A_t and Σ_t are all time-varying. The lag is chosen to be 1 due to the shortness of the time periods.

As for the impulse response functions, they are elaborated as that the size of the shock (impulse) corresponds to one standard deviation of the error term. The model is estimated for all the variables, examining at each estimation:

- The effect of Covid-19 shocks on ERIX returns
- The effect of Covid-19 shocks on Platinum returns
- The effect of Covid-19 shocks on Silver returns
- The effect of Covid-19 shocks on Gold returns
- The effect of Covid-19 shocks on Aluminum returns
- The effect of Covid-19 shocks on Corn returns
- The effect of Covid-19 shocks on Wheat returns
- The effect of Covid-19 shocks on Soybean returns.

Thus, the impulse variable is the variation of the number of Covid-19 global cases, while the response variables are the variations of the prices of ERIX, Platinum, Silver, Gold, Aluminum, Corn, Wheat and Soybean.

5 Empirical Results

5.1 Descriptive Statistics

The descriptive statistics are reported in Table 1. It shows the number of observations, Minimum, Maximum, Mean and standard deviations of both the dependent and independent variables. Panel 1 shows the results for the whole period; panel 2 shows the results for the first period and panel 3 shows the results for the second period. For the commodities, the findings show that Gold has the highest mean of 0.14% while corn has the lowest mean of −0.26% for the whole period. As for volatility, we find that the European Clean Energy Index is the most volatile with a standard deviation of 3.26%, while soybean is the least volatile with a standard deviation of 0.95%. During the first period, i.e. with the news about the sickness spreading all over the globe, Gold still the commodity with the highest mean of 0.2% while platinum turns to be the one with the smallest mean variation of −0.26%. ERIX and Soybean still the most and least volatile commodities consecutively. Yet, their volatility is lower than that of the whole period. After the announcement of Covid-19 as a pandemic, Gold remains the commodity with the highest mean variation (yet it is lower than that of the whole period and the first period), while corn turns to be the commodity with the lowest mean variation. As for volatility, Soybean holds its position as the least volatile commodity, while Platinum becomes the most volatile. After the Pandemic shock, volatilities are higher than the values recorded for the whole period and the first period.

Table 2 shows the results of the normality tests. The values reported are the statistics for skewness, excess kurtosis and Jarque-Bera test. The findings indicate that despite the transformation, the distribution of our data is still not normal. With ERIX, Platinum and silver being slightly negatively skewed and showing excess kurtosis surpassing 3. It is also the case for corn and aluminum (the latter has kurtosis smaller than 3, alongside with soybean). Overall, despite these results, the values of the statistics (skewness, kurtosis) are relatively close to those of the normal distribution. Figure 1.a shows the distribution of our variables.

Table 3 reports the results of the ADF Unit Root test. The findings show that despite the performed transformation of the variables, i.e., the data are still not stationary. The graphs of the returns are shown in Fig. 1b.

Table 1 Descriptive statistics

Variable	Observations	Min	Mean	Max	Std.dev
Panel 1: Whole period					
ERIX	78	−0.12408	−0.001427	0.11973	0.032653
PLATINIUM	78	−0.12014	−0.002128	0.10433	0.031807
SILVER	78	−0.14612	−0.0016682	0.079862	0.028678
GOLD	78	−0.037704	0.0014052	0.063334	0.01688
ALUMINUM	78	−0.045343	−0.0024052	0.039432	0.01405
CORN	78	−0.057307	−0.002684	0.032258	0.013267
WHEAT	78	−0.052101	−0.0015072	0.046211	0.015
SOYABEAN	78	−0.032297	−0.0016472	0.024706	0.0095502
COVID_GC	78	0	0.19132	2.6212	0.3931
Panel 2: Period 1					
ERIX	49	−0.067438	−0.0014412	0.048654	0.021023
PLATINIUM	49	−0.04112	−0.0026596	0.042782	0.016147
SILVER	49	−0.060972	−0.0015888	0.026458	0.014452
GOLD	49	−0.03227	0.0020647	0.030546	0.010181
ALUMINUM	49	−0.033022	−0.001514	0.021448	0.011889
CORN	49	−0.03125	−0.00047944	0.032258	0.011384
WHEAT	49	−0.052101	−0.0022765	0.031301	0.012535
SOYABEAN	49	−0.023918	−0.0017912	0.010357	0.0075203
COVID_GC	49	0	0.23905	2.6212	0.48493
Panel 3: Period 2					
ERIX	29	−0.12408	−0.0014031	0.11973	0.046054
PLATINIUM	29	−0.12014	−0.0012297	0.10433	0.047741
SILVER	29	−0.14612	−0.0018025	0.079862	0.043117
GOLD	29	−0.037704	0.000291	0.063334	0.024275
ALUMINUM	29	−0.045343	−0.0039108	0.039432	0.016986
CORN	29	−0.057307	−0.006409	0.018349	0.015244
WHEAT	29	−0.039116	−0.00020747	0.046211	0.018356
SOYABEAN	29	−0.032297	−0.0014037	0.024706	0.012234
COVID_GC	29	0.036731	0.11067	0.39515	0.089042

5.2 *Results Interpretation*

5.2.1 Impulse Response Functions

The impulse response functions are reported in Fig. 2. The graph shows the impulse response functions for each commodity for the whole period, the first period and the second period. Starting with ERIX, the figure shows an increase of the returns in the

Table 2 Normality tests

Normality test:	H0: p-value > 0,05: Normal distribution	
ERIX		
	Statistic	P-Value
Skewness	−0.27699	0.30889
Excess Kurtosis	3.6839	7.6418e−012
Jarque-Bera	45.103	1.6070e−010
Non-Normal Distribution (Reject H0)		
PLATINUM		
Skewness	−0.21116	0.43790
Excess Kurtosis	5.6502	8.7484e−026
Jarque-Bera	104.34	2.2073e−023
Non-Normal Distribution (Reject H0)		
SILVER		
Skewness	−1.1677	1.7898e−005
Excess Kurtosis	7.5825	4.4272e−045
Jarque-Bera	204.58	3.7677e−045
Non-Normal Distribution (Reject H0)		
GOLD		
Skewness	0.71705	0.0084346
Excess Kurtosis	2.1773	5.2183e−005
Jarque-Bera	22.091	1.5963e−005
Non-Normal Distribution (Reject H0)		
ALUMINUM		
Skewness	−0.44483	0.10223
Excess Kurtosis	1.0344	0.054596
Jarque-Bera	6.0498	0.048561
Non-Normal Distribution (Reject H0)		
CORN		
Skewness	−0.76746	0.0048119
Excess Kurtosis	3.1367	5.5954e−009
Jarque-Bera	39.634	2.4754e−009
Non-Normal Distribution (Reject H0)		
WHEAT		
Skewness	0.13037	0.63199
Excess Kurtosis	2.4260	6.5501e−006
Jarque-Bera	19.349	6.2876e−005
Non-Normal Distribution (Reject H0)		

(continued)

Table 2 (continued)

Normality test:	H0: p-value > 0,05: Normal distribution	
SOYBEAN		
Skewness	−0.29351	0.28093
Excess Kurtosis	1.8103	0.00076901
Jarque-Bera	11.770	0.0027803
Non-Normal Distribution (Reject H0)		
COVID_GC		
Skewness	4.6626	9.0941e−066
Excess Kurtosis	23.662	0.00000
Jarque-Bera	2102.2	0.00000
Non-Normal Distribution (Reject H0)		

first period, due to the shock coming from the spread of the Coronavirus. After the declaration of Covid-19 as a pandemic, ERIX prices rose higher than the first period with a more persistent shock. The magnitude of the shock during the second period was larger than that of the whole period. Regarding platinum, the shock coming from the increase if the number of Covid-19 global cases pushed prices down in the first period, then they turned higher in the second period. Again, the shock of the second period is steeper and more persistent. As for silver, the impulse response functions show a slight increase in its returns which has the same pattern for the first period and the second period. The shock decays within a three-day time lapse. Gold returns start negative in the first period. The shock has a sharper magnitude than that of the whole period and it decays within a 4-day period. After the announcement of the pandemic, Gold prices rose; this is translated by the increase of returns shown in Fig. 2d, yet the shock was not very sharp. This could be explained by the nature of Gold as a safe-haven commodity in times of crises. Due to the outspread of the pandemic, investors predicted a drop in stock prices, which is normally accompanied by a rise in Gold prices used as a safe-haven. As for Aluminum, the prices did not respond to the coronavirus shock during the first period, yet the returns were negative during the second period. Corn and wheat returns responded positively during the first period and did not respond in the second period. As for soybean, the response is like that of Gold. A negative response during the first period and a positive one during the second period.

One explanation to these results is that commodities are considered as hedging tools when stock prices fall during crises. For this reason, most of them show an increase in prices and returns during the second period, i.e. after the announcement of Covid-19 as a pandemic. This is mostly known for precious metals, such as Gold and platinum. The decrease in their returns in the first period is explained by the fact that with the spread of the news about the coronavirus, investors predict a sharp rise in prices when it spreads worldwide. Thus they will hold them, waiting for the prices to rise later to sell. For the ERIX index, renewable energies are a substitute

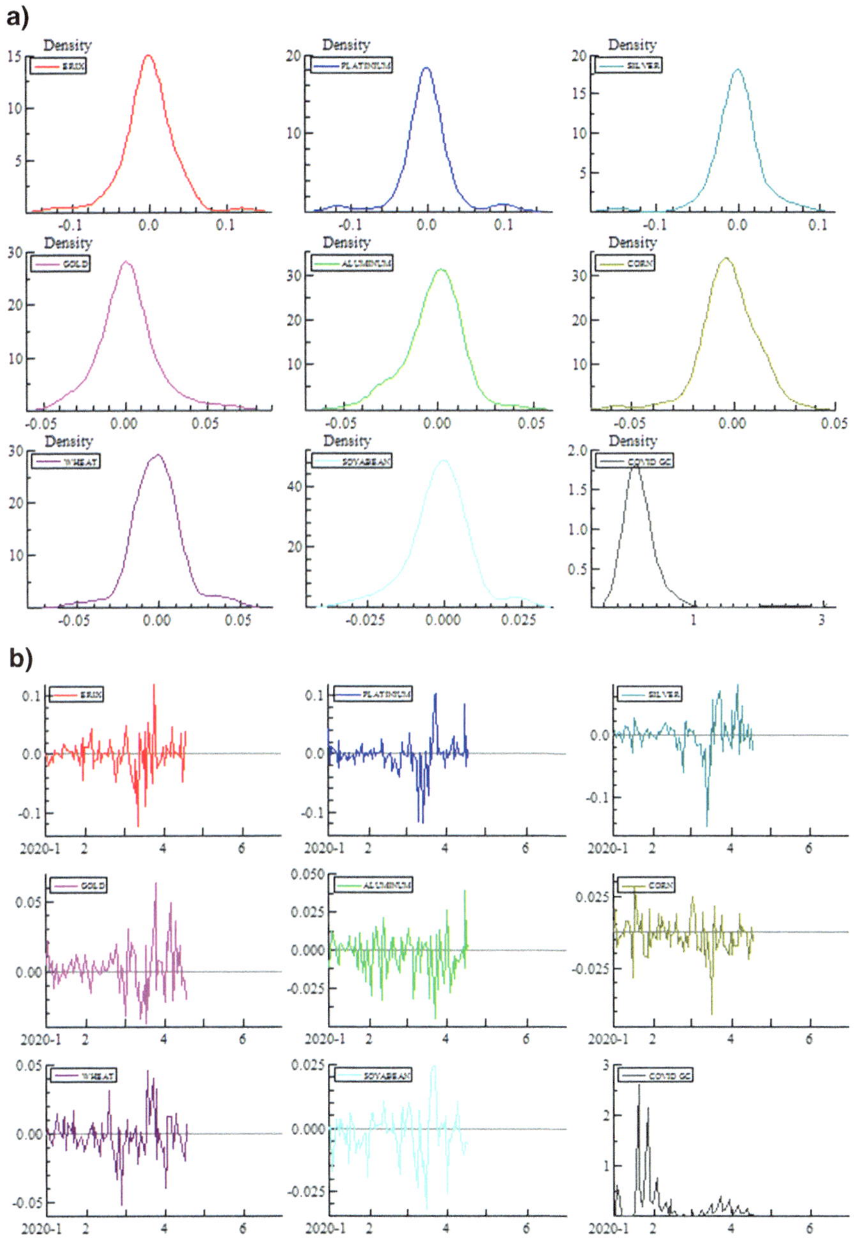

Fig. 1 Distributions and returns plots: **a.** Distribution plots. **b.** Return plots

Table 3 ADF unit root test

	Asymptotic critical values	Stationarity	
ADF Statistics	1%	5%	10%
	−2.56572	−1.94093	−1.61663
ERIX	−5.7108	Not Stationary	
PLATINIUM	−5.22825	Not Stationary	
SILVER	−4.3717	Not Stationary	
GOLD	−5.44344	Not Stationary	
ALUMINUM	−7.46478	Not Stationary	
CORN	−6.26641	Not Stationary	
–	−4.67166	Not Stationary	
SOYABEAN	−4.45539	Not Stationary	
COVID_GC	−4.1891	Not Stationary	

for classical fossil energy commodities (such as oil and gas) which are known to respond negatively to such shocks. Consequently, a reverse response is seen. As for agricultural commodities (Corn and Wheat), the response could be explained by the fact that investors hold them to hedge the risk of their portfolios, thus their demand rose in the first period, as the aim is to hold them in the portfolio and not to make profit out of the crisis such as precious metals. These features are shown in the prices graphs, reported in Fig. 3.

5.2.2 Stochastic Volatility

The stochastic volatility graphs are reported in Fig. 4. The graphs show the stochastic volatility for the 5%, 50% and 95% later quantiles for the whole period, the first period and the second period. The findings show that all commodities are more volatile in the second period, i.e. after the announcement of Covid-19 as a pandemic. These results go along with those found in the impulse response functions. The shocks were sharper in the second period and decayed slower. Agricultural commodities (wheat and soybeans) are the least volatile, which goes with our earlier interpretation of their use for hedging portfolios risk. They are followed by precious metals, since their demand varies during times of crises. They are requested in these times as their prices rise, to make profits that cover the losses coming from equities. ERIX is found to be the most volatile commodity. This result is expected since it would behave as an energy commodity and its supply and demand get affected by crises.

5.2.3 Variance Decomposition

The results of the variance decomposition with a forecast length of 15 days are reported in Table 4. Each panel shows the contribution of the variation of the number of Covid-19 global cases to the returns of various commodities. The variance decomposition was extracted by re-estimating the model using a basic VAR model.

The findings show that apart from their own shocks, all the commodities reacted to the change in coronavirus global cases shock. In fact, the participation of the variance

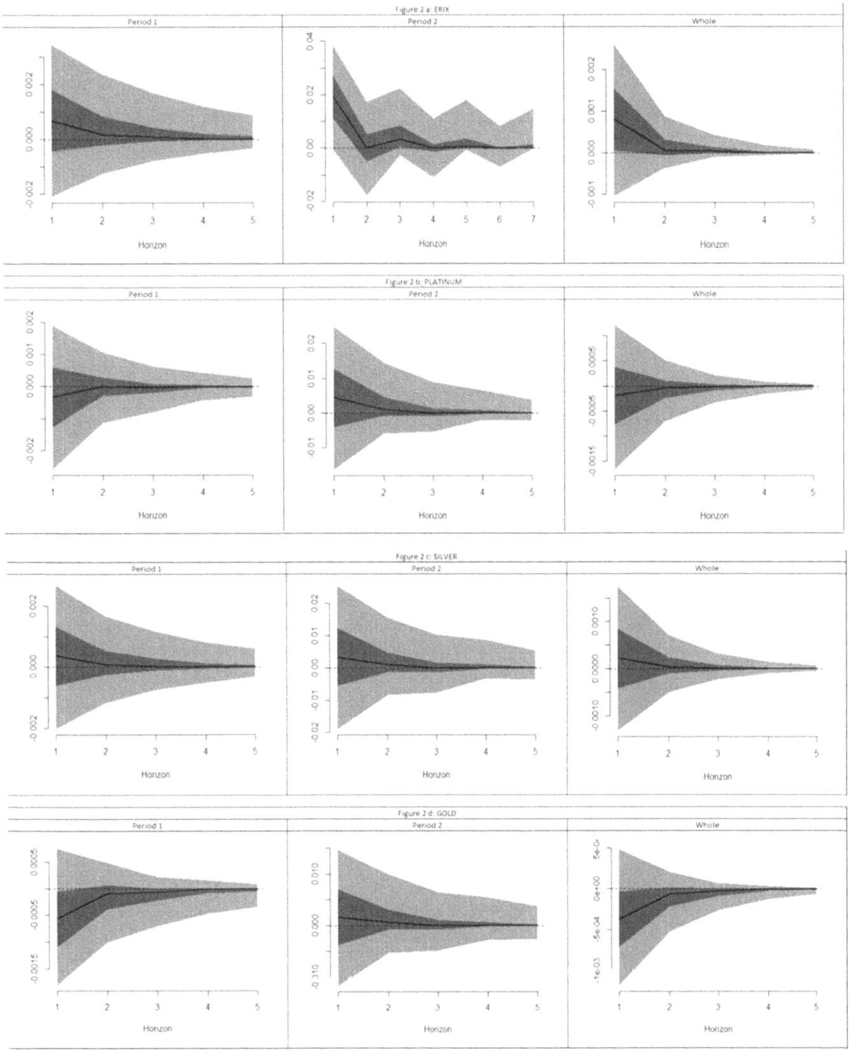

Fig. 2 Impulse response functions

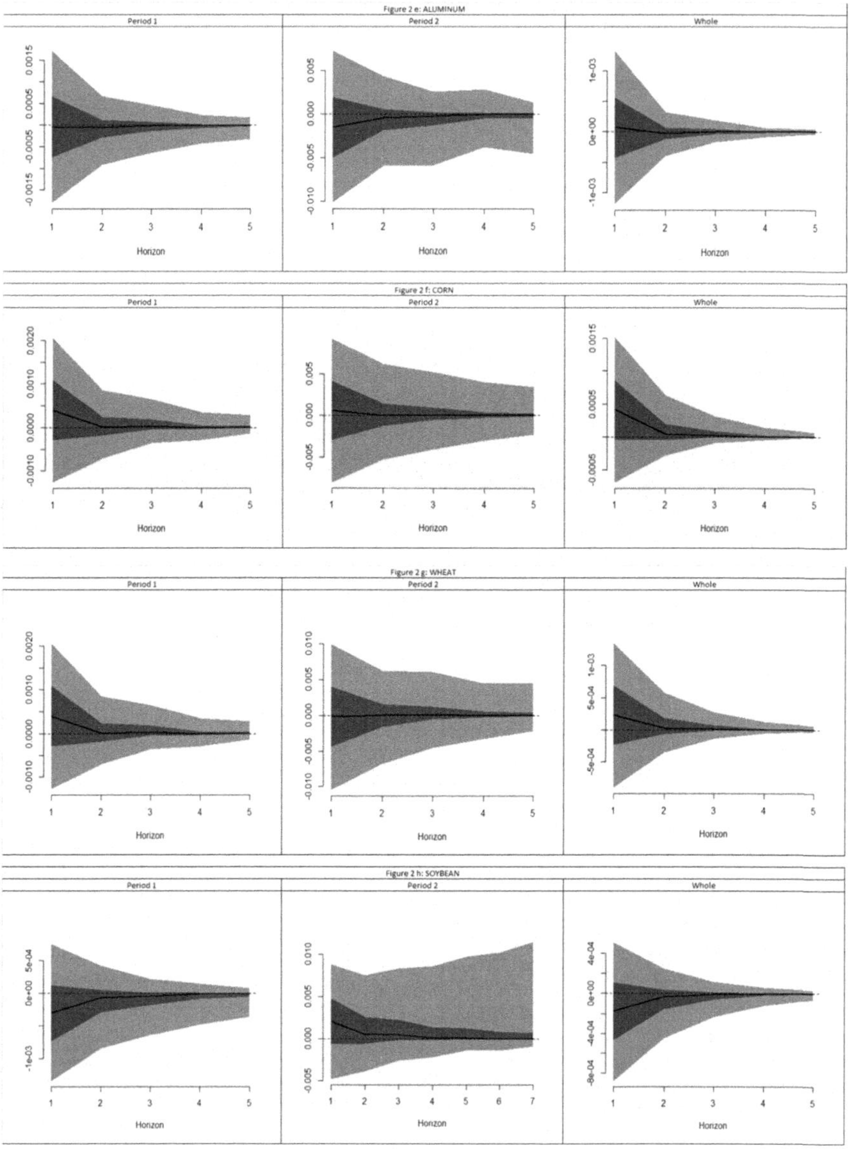

Fig. 2 (continued)

coming from the coronavirus shock gets higher in the first period compared to the whole period and gets even higher during the second period (after the announcement of Covid-19 as a pandemic) except for corn. Moreover, the part of the variance of Covid-19 variation remains persistent until the 15th day of the forecast. During the second period, ERIX reacted the most with a contribution of 32% of Covid-19

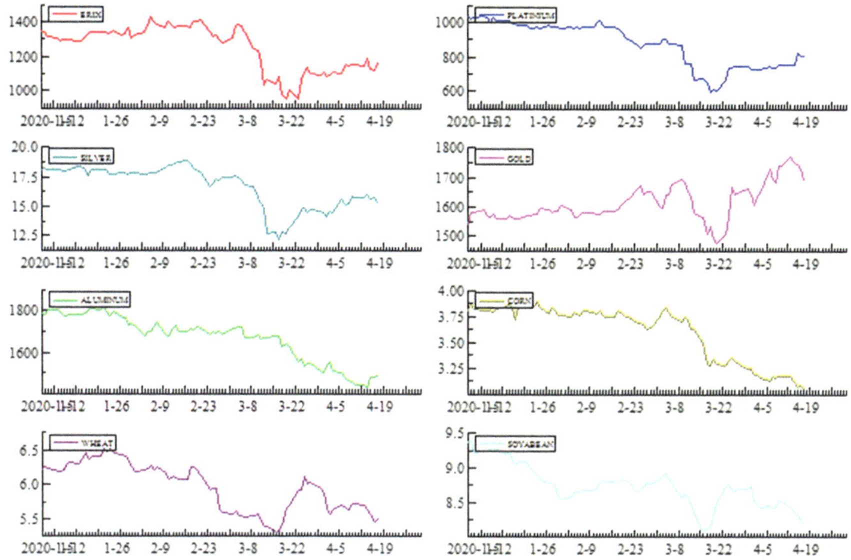

Fig. 3 Prices plots

variation in its variance, followed by precious metals (silver 15%, platinum 14%, aluminum 16% and Gold 12%). Agricultural commodities follow Covid-19 changes reaching 0.049% for soybean, 0.042% for wheat and 0.026% for corn.

These results strengthen up our findings even more, suggesting that it is better to use metal commodities to make profit during crises, by buying them when an event is expected and then selling when that event really occurs to benefit from the price upward variation and compensate losses. While agricultural commodities are better to use as a mean for hedging portfolio's risk due to their low affection by these shocks.

6 Conclusion

In this chapter, we have analyzed the implications of Covid-19 pandemic on the returns of the European renewable energy Index and the most relevant precious metals and agricultural commodity prices. The period spanned by our data goes from 02 January 2020 to 17 April 2020. The data sample is divided into two sub-periods, before and after the announcement of the pandemic by WHO. Using a TVP-VAR model, our analysis shows that the reaction of commodity markets to Covid-19 shocks varies from one period to another. In particular, our results indicate that except Aluminum, the spread of Covid-19 Pandemic has a significantly positive influence

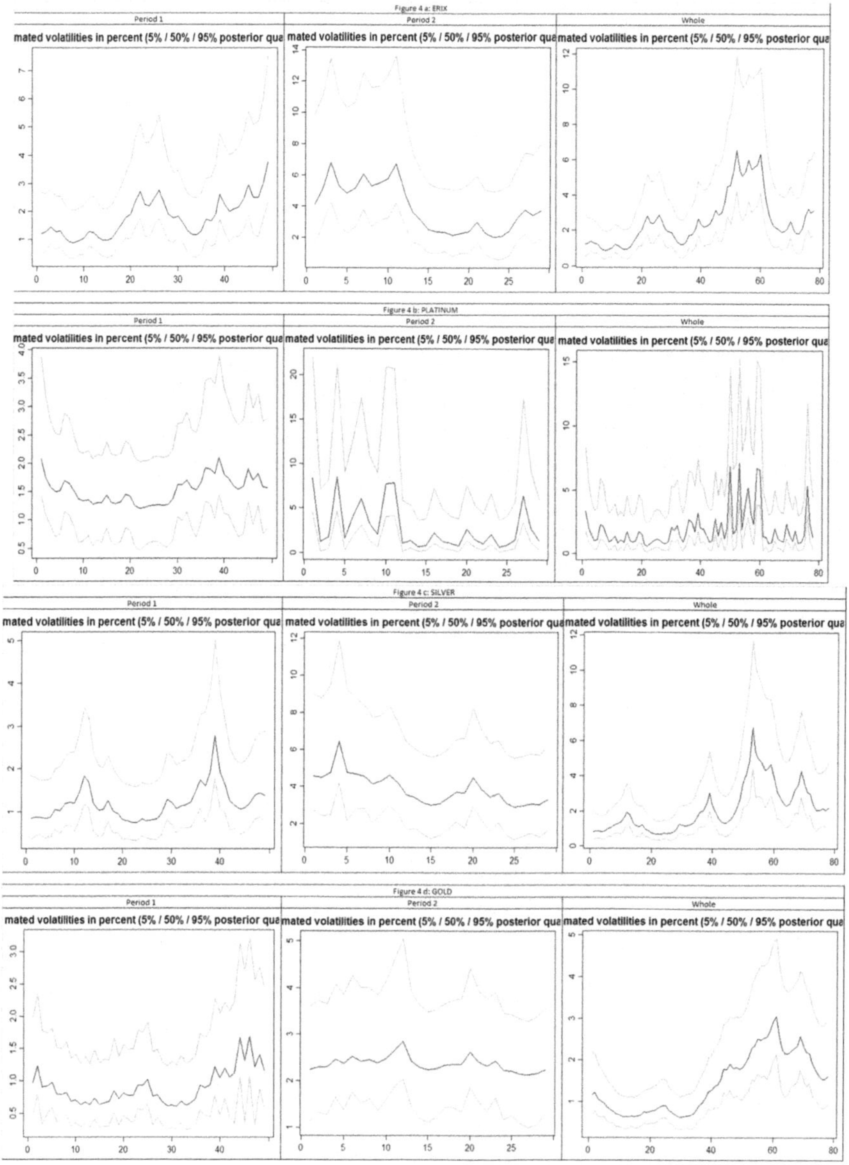

Fig. 4 Stochastic volatility

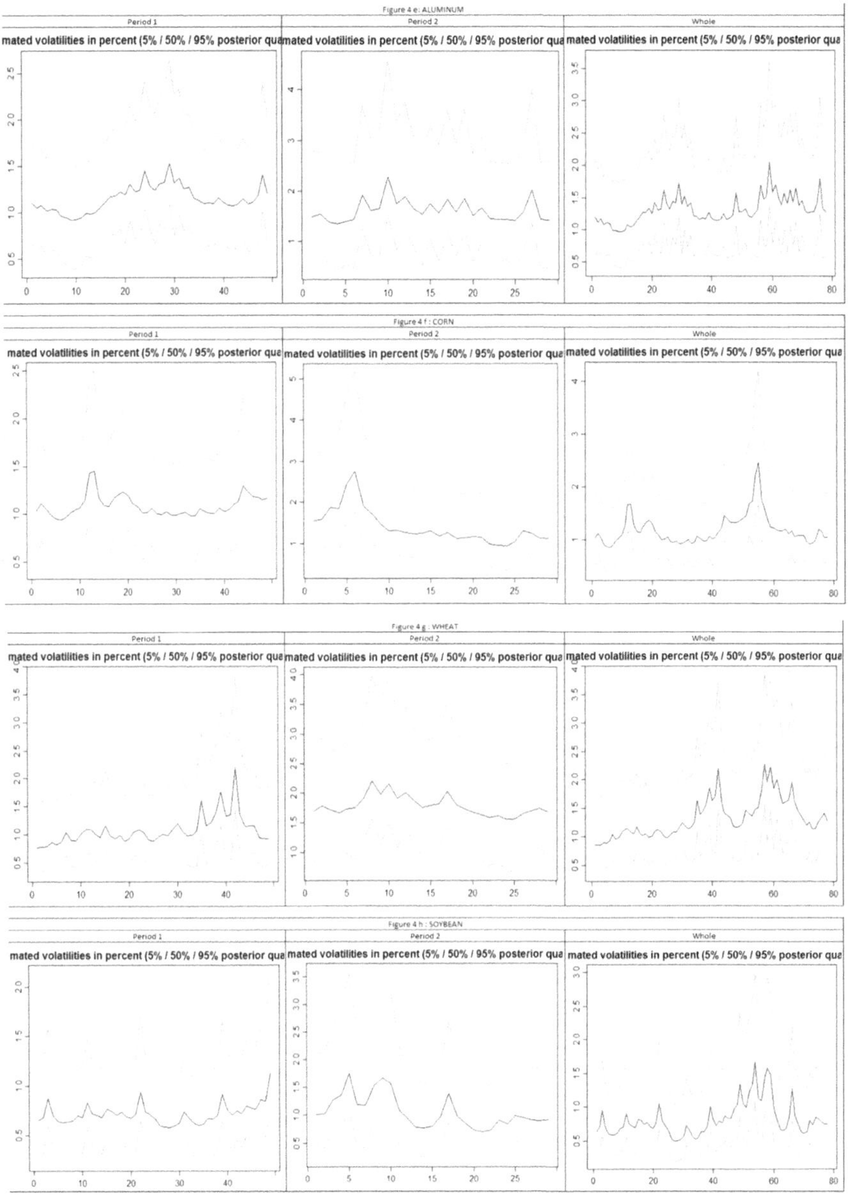

Fig. 4 (continued)

Table 4 Variance decomposition

Panel 1: ERIX

	Period 1	Period 2	Whole			
Forecast	COVID	ERIX	COVID	ERIX	COVID	ERIX
1	0.00742457	0.9925754	0.02734406	0.9726559	0.003993891	0.9960061
2	0.01973482	0.9802652	0.32142140	0.6785786	0.019200161	0.9807998
3	0.02239755	0.9776024	0.31796567	0.6820343	0.019864715	0.9801353
4	0.02275551	0.9772445	0.32132987	0.6786701	0.019932827	0.9800672
5	0.02279832	0.9772017	0.32127225	0.6787277	0.019938412	0.9800616
6	0.02280327	0.9771967	0.32132823	0.6786718	0.019938895	0.9800611
7	0.02280384	0.9771962	0.32132729	0.6786727	0.019938936	0.9800611
8	0.02280390	0.9771961	0.32132823	0.6786718	0.019938939	0.9800611
9	0.02280391	0.9771961	0.32132821	0.6786718	0.019938940	0.9800611
10	0.02280391	0.9771961	0.32132823	0.6786718	0.019938940	0.9800611
11	0.02280391	0.9771961	0.32132823	0.6786718	0.019938940	0.9800611
12	0.02280391	0.9771961	0.32132823	0.6786718	0.019938940	0.9800611
13	0.02280391	0.9771961	0.32132823	0.6786718	0.019938940	0.9800611
14	0.02280391	0.9771961	0.32132823	0.6786718	0.019938940	0.9800611
15	0.02280391	0.9771961	0.32132823	0.6786718	0.019938940	0.9800611

(continued)

Table 4 (continued)

Panel 2: PLATINUM

	Period 1	Period 2	Whole			
Forecast	COVID	PLATINUM	COVID	PLATINUM	COVID	PLATINUM
1	0.03834501	0.9616550	0.1188103	0.8811897	0.01359146	0.9864085
2	0.04622216	0.9537778	0.1491826	0.8508174	0.01360710	0.9863929
3	0.04664001	0.9533600	0.1497605	0.8502395	0.01368462	0.9863154
4	0.04667024	0.9533298	0.1497556	0.8502444	0.01369367	0.9863063
5	0.04667237	0.9533276	0.1497566	0.8502434	0.01369446	0.9863055
6	0.04667252	0.9533275	0.1497566	0.8502434	0.01369452	0.9863055
7	0.04667253	0.9533275	0.1497566	0.8502434	0.01369453	0.9863055
8	0.04667253	0.9533275	0.1497566	0.8502434	0.01369453	0.9863055
9	0.04667253	0.9533275	0.1497566	0.8502434	0.01369453	0.9863055
10	0.04667253	0.9533275	0.1497566	0.8502434	0.01369453	0.9863055
11	0.04667253	0.9533275	0.1497566	0.8502434	0.01369453	0.9863055
12	0.04667253	0.9533275	0.1497566	0.8502434	0.01369453	0.9863055
13	0.04667253	0.9533275	0.1497566	0.8502434	0.01369453	0.9863055
14	0.04667253	0.9533275	0.1497566	0.8502434	0.01369453	0.9863055
15	0.04667253	0.9533275	0.1497566	0.8502434	0.01369453	0.9863055

(continued)

Table 4 (continued)

Panel 3: SILVER						
	Period 1	Period 2	Whole			
Forecast	COVID	SILVER	COVID	SILVER	COVID	SILVER
1	0.006239224	0.9937608	0.1524300	0.8475700	0.008201460	0.9917985
2	0.010490631	0.9895094	0.1594780	0.8405220	0.009704673	0.9902953
3	0.010983254	0.9890167	0.1594893	0.8405107	0.009818897	0.9901811
4	0.011029299	0.9889707	0.1594893	0.8405107	0.009826939	0.9901731
5	0.011033411	0.9889666	0.1594893	0.8405107	0.009827501	0.9901725
6	0.011033775	0.9889662	0.1594893	0.8405107	0.009827541	0.9901725
7	0.011033807	0.9889662	0.1594893	0.8405107	0.009827543	0.9901725
8	0.011033810	0.9889662	0.1594893	0.8405107	0.009827543	0.9901725
9	0.011033810	0.9889662	0.1594893	0.8405107	0.009827543	0.9901725
10	0.011033810	0.9889662	0.1594893	0.8405107	0.009827543	0.9901725
11	0.011033810	0.9889662	0.1594893	0.8405107	0.009827543	0.9901725
12	0.011033810	0.9889662	0.1594893	0.8405107	0.009827543	0.9901725
13	0.011033810	0.9889662	0.1594893	0.8405107	0.009827543	0.9901725
14	0.011033810	0.9889662	0.1594893	0.8405107	0.009827543	0.9901725
15	0.011033810	0.9889662	0.1594893	0.8405107	0.009827543	0.9901725

(continued)

Table 4 (continued)

Panel 4: GOLD

	Period 1	Period 2	Whole			
Forecast	COVID	GOLD	COVID	GOLD	COVID	GOLD
1	0.002097672	0.9979023	0.1172074	0.8827926	0.004681231	0.9953188
2	0.033080477	0.9669195	0.1205299	0.8794701	0.009021056	0.9909789
3	0.035563249	0.9644368	0.1205875	0.8794125	0.009589466	0.9904105
4	0.035633177	0.9643668	0.1205877	0.8794123	0.009631913	0.9903681
5	0.035633720	0.9643663	0.1205877	0.8794123	0.009634620	0.9903654
6	0.035633722	0.9643663	0.1205877	0.8794123	0.009634783	0.9903652
7	0.035633723	0.9643663	0.1205877	0.8794123	0.009634793	0.9903652
8	0.035633723	0.9643663	0.1205877	0.8794123	0.009634793	0.9903652
9	0.035633723	0.9643663	0.1205877	0.8794123	0.009634793	0.9903652
10	0.035633723	0.9643663	0.1205877	0.8794123	0.009634793	0.9903652
11	0.035633723	0.9643663	0.1205877	0.8794123	0.009634793	0.9903652
12	0.035633723	0.9643663	0.1205877	0.8794123	0.009634793	0.9903652
13	0.035633723	0.9643663	0.1205877	0.8794123	0.009634793	0.9903652
14	0.035633723	0.9643663	0.1205877	0.8794123	0.009634793	0.9903652
15	0.035633723	0.9643663	0.1205877	0.8794123	0.009634793	0.9903652

(continued)

Table 4 (continued)

Panel 5: ALUMINUM

	Period 1	Period 2	Whole			
Forecast	COVID	ALUMINUM	COVID	ALUMINUM	COVID	ALUMINUM
1	0.02087538	0.9791246	0.1711854	0.8288146	0.01419102	0.9858090
2	0.02020859	0.9797914	0.1647333	0.8352667	0.01374500	0.9862550
3	0.02022884	0.9797712	0.1631389	0.8368611	0.01375701	0.9862430
4	0.02022829	0.9797717	0.1629471	0.8370529	0.01375639	0.9862436
5	0.02022838	0.9797716	0.1629209	0.8370791	0.01375644	0.9862436
6	0.02022838	0.9797716	0.1629174	0.8370826	0.01375644	0.9862436
7	0.02022838	0.9797716	0.1629169	0.8370831	0.01375644	0.9862436
8	0.02022838	0.9797716	0.1629169	0.8370831	0.01375644	0.9862436
9	0.02022838	0.9797716	0.1629169	0.8370831	0.01375644	0.9862436
10	0.02022838	0.9797716	0.1629169	0.8370831	0.01375644	0.9862436
11	0.02022838	0.9797716	0.1629169	0.8370831	0.01375644	0.9862436
12	0.02022838	0.9797716	0.1629169	0.8370831	0.01375644	0.9862436
13	0.02022838	0.9797716	0.1629169	0.8370831	0.01375644	0.9862436
14	0.02022838	0.9797716	0.1629169	0.8370831	0.01375644	0.9862436
15	0.02022838	0.9797716	0.1629169	0.8370831	0.01375644	0.9862436

(continued)

Table 4 (continued)

Panel 6: CORN						
	Period 1	Period 2	Whole			
Forecast	COVID	CORN	COVID	CORN	COVID	CORN
1	0.03398758	0.9660124	0.02248374	0.9775163	0.02303467	0.9769653
2	0.04615500	0.9538450	0.02582090	0.9741791	0.03356377	0.9664362
3	0.04631171	0.9536883	0.02624220	0.9737578	0.03517370	0.9648263
4	0.04638535	0.9536147	0.02626941	0.9737306	0.03540316	0.9645968
5	0.04639159	0.9536084	0.02627094	0.9737291	0.03543588	0.9645641
6	0.04639252	0.9536075	0.02627102	0.9737290	0.03544054	0.9645595
7	0.04639263	0.9536074	0.02627102	0.9737290	0.03544121	0.9645588
8	0.04639264	0.9536074	0.02627102	0.9737290	0.03544130	0.9645587
9	0.04639264	0.9536074	0.02627102	0.9737290	0.03544132	0.9645587
10	0.04639264	0.9536074	0.02627102	0.9737290	0.03544132	0.9645587
11	0.04639264	0.9536074	0.02627102	0.9737290	0.03544132	0.9645587
12	0.04639264	0.9536074	0.02627102	0.9737290	0.03544132	0.9645587
13	0.04639264	0.9536074	0.02627102	0.9737290	0.03544132	0.9645587
14	0.04639264	0.9536074	0.02627102	0.9737290	0.03544132	0.9645587
15	0.04639264	0.9536074	0.02627102	0.9737290	0.03544132	0.9645587

(continued)

Table 4 (continued)

Panel 7: WHEAT

	Period 1	Period 2	Whole			
Forecast	COVID	WHEAT	COVID	WHEAT	COVID	WHEAT
1	7.310777e−06	0.9999927	0.04427443	0.9557256	9.517131e−05	0.9999048
2	1.444339e−02	0.9855566	0.04260862	0.9573914	4.162395e−03	0.9958376
3	1.548244e−02	0.9845176	0.04263314	0.9573669	4.763103e−03	0.9952369
4	1.555695e−02	0.9844430	0.04263503	0.9573650	4.820581e−03	0.9951794
5	1.556230e−02	0.9844377	0.04263507	0.9573649	4.825385e−03	0.9951746
6	1.556269e−02	0.9844373	0.04263507	0.9573649	4.825767e−03	0.9951742
7	1.556271e−02	0.9844373	0.04263507	0.9573649	4.825797e−03	0.9951742
8	1.556272e−02	0.9844373	0.04263507	0.9573649	4.825800e−03	0.9951742
9	1.556272e−02	0.9844373	0.04263507	0.9573649	4.825800e−03	0.9951742
10	1.556272e−02	0.9844373	0.04263507	0.9573649	4.825800e−03	0.9951742
11	1.556272e−02	0.9844373	0.04263507	0.9573649	4.825800e−03	0.9951742
12	1.556272e−02	0.9844373	0.04263507	0.9573649	4.825800e−03	0.9951742
13	1.556272e−02	0.9844373	0.04263507	0.9573649	4.825800e−03	0.9951742
14	1.556272e−02	0.9844373	0.04263507	0.9573649	4.825800e−03	0.9951742
15	1.556272e−02	0.9844373	0.04263507	0.9573649	4.825800e−03	0.9951742

(continued)

Table 4 (continued)

Panel 8: SOYBEAN						
	Period 1	Period 2	Whole			
Forecast	COVID	SOYBEAN	COVID	SOYBEAN	COVID	SOYBEAN
1	0.002603566	0.9973964	0.005917027	0.9940830	0.0009468477	0.9990532
2	0.013422384	0.9865776	0.041907977	0.9580920	0.0028748772	0.9971251
3	0.014884152	0.9851158	0.047602092	0.9523979	0.0033672748	0.9966327
4	0.015012300	0.9849877	0.049129338	0.9508707	0.0034489459	0.9965511
5	0.015021887	0.9849781	0.049537997	0.9504620	0.0034598770	0.9965401
6	0.015022557	0.9849774	0.049649393	0.9503506	0.0034611674	0.9965388
7	0.015022602	0.9849774	0.049679834	0.9503202	0.0034613075	0.9965387
8	0.015022605	0.9849774	0.049688162	0.9503118	0.0034613219	0.9965387
9	0.015022605	0.9849774	0.049690440	0.9503096	0.0034613233	0.9965387
10	0.015022605	0.9849774	0.049691064	0.9503089	0.0034613234	0.9965387
11	0.015022605	0.9849774	0.049691234	0.9503088	0.0034613234	0.9965387
12	0.015022605	0.9849774	0.049691281	0.9503087	0.0034613234	0.9965387
13	0.015022605	0.9849774	0.049691294	0.9503087	0.0034613234	0.9965387
14	0.015022605	0.9849774	0.049691297	0.9503087	0.0034613234	0.9965387
15	0.015022605	0.9849774	0.049691298	0.9503087	0.0034613234	0.9965387

on the returns of renewable clean energy stocks and most precious metals (Platinum, Silver, and Gold) after the announcement of Covid-19 as a pandemic. However, apart Soybeans which had a similar reaction to Gold, agricultural commodities (Corn and Wheat) did not respond to Covid-19 outbreak. Our findings also show that renewable energy stocks are the most volatile after the announcement of the pandemic, whereas, agriculture commodities are the least volatile. In addition to that, the results of the variance decomposition showing the higher reaction of renewable energy and the weak reaction of agriculture commodities document the safe haven capability of Gold and the hedging properties of some precious metals and agriculture commodities in period of financial distress. However, the uncertainty around the current Covid-19 pandemic may persist for an extended period leading to long-term declines in various commodity prices. The deepening economic contraction with continuing mitigation measures may further reduce the global supply and demand for non-energy and metal commodities. Governments worldwide should adopt important policy actions in order to guaranty price stability of different commodities during periods of Covid-19 pandemic.

References

Bakas D, Triantafyllou A (2018) The impact of uncertainty shocks on the volatility of commodity prices. J Int Money Finance 87:96–111. https://doi.org/10.1016/j.jimonfin.2018.06.001

Bakas D, Triantafyllou A (2020) Commodity price volatility and the economic uncertainty of pandemics. Econ Lett 193:109283. https://doi.org/10.1016/j.econlet.2020.109283

Baldwin, R., & di Mauro, B. W. (2020). Economics in the Time of COVID-19.A VoxEU.org Book. London: Centre for Economic Policy Research Press

Baldwin R, Tomiura E (2020) Thinking ahead about the trade impact of COVID-19. A VoxEU.org Book. Centre for Economic Policy Research Press, London

Birol F (2020) Put clean energy at the heart of stimulus plans to counter the coronavirus crisis—Analysis—IEA. IEA, (pp 1–4). Retrieved 21 April, from https://www.iea.org/commentaries/put-clean-energy-at-the-heart-of-stimulus-plans-to-counter-the-coronavirus-crisis

Bloom DE, Cadarette D, Sevilla JP (2018) Epidemics and economics: New and resurgent infectious diseases can have far-reaching economic repercussions. Finance Dev 55(2):46–49

Cabrera BL, Schulz F (2016) Volatility linkages between energy and agricultural commodity prices. Energy Econ 54:190–203

Chen MP, Lee CC, Lin YH, Chen WY (2018) Did the SARS epidemic weaken the integration of asian stock markets? Evidence from smooth time-varying cointegration analysis. Econ Res -EkonomskaIstraživanja 31(1):908–926

Conlon T, McGee R (2020) Safe haven or risky hazard? Bitcoin during the COVID-19 bear market. Finance Res Lett 35

Corbet S, Larkin C, Lucey B (2020) The contagion effects of the COVID-19 pandemic: evidence from gold and cryptocurrencies. Finance Res Lett 35:101554. https://doi.org/10.1016/j.frl.2020.101554

Dahl RE, Oglend A, Yahya M (2019) Dynamics of volatility spillover in commodity markets: linking crude oil to agriculture. J Commod Markets. 100111. https://doi.org/10.1016/j.jcomm.2019.100111

Del Negro M, Primiceri GE (2015) Time varying structural vector autoregressions and monetary policy: a corrigendum. Rev Econ Stud 82(4):1342–1345

Elnahas A, Kim D, Kim I (2018) Natural disaster risk and corporate leverage
Emma N (2020) Coronavirus could weaken climate change action, hit clean energy. Retrieved 21 April 2020, from https://www.cnbc.com/2020/03/13/coronavirus-could-weaken-climate-change-action-hitclean-energy.html
Gautam S (2020) The influence of COVID-19 on air quality in India: a boon or inutile. Bull Environ Contam Toxicol 0123456789:2019–2021. https://doi.org/10.1007/s00128-020-02877-y
Goodell JW (2020) COVID-19 and finance: agendas for future research. Finance Res Lett 101512. https://doi.org/10.1016/j.frl.2020.101512
Gupta A, Bherwani H, Gautam S, Anjum S, Musugu K, Kumar N et al (2020) Air pollution aggravating COVID-19 lethality? Exploration in Asian cities using statistical models. Environ Dev Sustain. https://doi.org/10.1007/s10668-020-008789
Kang SH, McIver R, Yoon S-M (2017) Dynamic spillover effects among crude oil, precious metal, and agricultural commodity futures markets. Energy Econ 62:19–32
Koirala KH, Mishra AK, D'Antoni JM, Mehlhorn JE (2015) Energy prices and agricultural commodity prices: testing correlation using copulas method. Energy 81:430–436. https://doi.org/10.1016/j.energy.2014.12.055
Leoni PL (2013) HIV/AIDS and banking stability in developing countries. Bull Econ Res 65(3):225–237. https://doi.org/10.1111/j.1467-8586.2011.00401.x
Mann CL (2020) Real and financial lenses to assess the economic consequences of COVID-19. A VoxEU.org Book. Centre for Economic Policy Research Press, London
McPhee D (2020) Moray east offshore wind project 'on track' despite Covid-19 delays, director claims. Energy Voice. Retrieved 21 April 2020, from https://www.energyvoice.com/otherenergy/235798/moray-east-offshore-wind-project-on-track-despite-covid-19-delays-director-claims/
Meninno R, Wolff G (2020) As coronavirus spreads, can the EU afford to close its borders? In: Baldwin R, di Mauro BW (eds) Economics in the time of COVID-19. CEPR Press
Primiceri GE (2005) Time varying structural vector autoregressions and monetary policy. Rev Econ Stud 72(3):821–852
Prokopczuk M, Stancu A, Symeonidis L (2019) The economic drivers of commodity market volatility. J Int Money Finan 98:102063. https://doi.org/10.1016/j.jimonfin.2019.102063
Reboredo JC (2012) Do food and oil prices co-move? Energy policy, 49:456–467. https://doi.org/10.1016/j.enpol.2012.06.035
Salisu AA, Akanni L, Raheem I (2020a) The COVID-19 global fear index and the predictability of commodity price returns. J Behav Exp Finan 100383. https://doi.org/10.1016/j.jbef.2020.100383
Salisu AA, Ebuh GU, Usman N (2020b) Revisiting oil-stock nexus during COVID-19 pandemic: some preliminary results. Int Rev Econ Finan 69:269–284. https://doi.org/10.1016/j.iref.2020.06.023
SEIA (2020a) Retrieved April 21, 2020, from https://www.seia.org/sites/default/files/2020-04/2020-April-SEIA-COVID-Factsheet.pdf
Serra T (2011) Volatility spillovers between food and energy markets: A semiparametric approach. Energy Econ 33(6):1155–1164. https://doi.org/10.1016/j.eneco.2011.04.003
Sharif A, Aloui C, Yarovaya L (2020) COVID-19 pandemic, oil prices, stock market, geopolitical risk and policy uncertainty nexus in the US economy: Fresh evidence from the wavelet-based approach. Int Rev Finan Anal 101496
Tiwari AK, Nasreen S, Shahbaz M, Hammoudeh S (2020) Time-frequency causality and connectedness between international prices of energy, food, industry, agriculture and metals. Energy Econ 85:104529. https://doi.org/10.1016/j.eneco.2019.104529
Wang J, Shao W, Kim J (2020) Analysis of the impact of COVID-19 on the correlations between crude oil and agricultural futures. Chaos, Solitons Fractals, 109896. https://doi.org/10.1016/j.chaos.2020.109896
WHO (2020) World health organization. World Health Organization, press conference on novel corona virus outbreak

World Bank (2019) Commodity markets outlook; The Role of substitution in commodity demand. October. World Bank, Washington, DC

World Bank (2020) Global economic prospects: the turning of the tide?. World Bank, Washington, DC

Yahya M, Oglend A, Dahl RE (2019) Temporal and spectral dependence between crude oil and agricultural commodities: a wavelet-based copula approach. Energy Econ 80:277–296. https://doi.org/10.1016/j.eneco.2019.01.011

Yip PS, Brooks R, Do HX, Nguyen DK (2020) Dynamic volatility spillover effects between oil and agricultural products. Int Rev Finan Anal 101465. https://doi.org/10.1016/j.irfa.2020.101465

Yosra Ghabri holds a Ph.D. in Finance from IHEC Carthage, Tunisia in 2017. She is currently an Assistant Professor of Finance at Carthage Business School, University of Tunis Carthage. Her teaching interests include Portfolio Management, Corporate Finance, Financial Markets and Financial Management. Her research areas are Corporate Governance, Market Microstructure, Portfolio Management and Energy Economics.

Ahmed Ayadi holds a research master degree in Finance from IHEC Carthage, Tunisia in 2017. He started working for Banque de Tunisie in October 2017 as a loan officer. He is currently a credit analyst for SMEs at Banque de Tunisie and a joint Ph.D. (in finance) student in IHEC Carthage, Tunisia and University of Paris 8| Vincennes—Saint Denis, France. His research area is financial contagion.

Printed by Printforce, the Netherlands